DO WHAT MATTERS MOST

DO WHAT MATTERS MOST

LEAD A LIFE BY **DESIGN**, NOT BY **DEFAULT**

SECOND EDITION

ROB SHALLENBERGER &
STEVE SHALLENBERGER

Berrett–Koehler Publishers, Inc.

Berrett-Koehler Publishers, Inc.
1333 Broadway, Suite P100
Oakland, CA 94612-1921
Tel: (510) 817-2277
Fax: (510) 817-2278
bkconnection.com

ORDERING INFORMATION
Quantity sales. Special discounts are available on quantity purchases by corporations, associations, and others. For details, please go to bkconnection.com to see our bulk discounts or contact bookorders@bkpub.com for more information.
Individual sales. Berrett-Koehler publications are available through most bookstores. They can also be ordered directly from Berrett-Koehler: Tel: (800) 929-2929; Fax: (802) 864-7626; bkconnection.com.
Orders for college textbook / course adoption use. Please contact Berrett-Koehler: Tel: (800) 929-2929; Fax: (802) 864-7626.

Distributed to the US trade and internationally by Penguin Random House Publisher Services.

Printed in the United States of America

Berrett-Koehler books are printed on long-lasting acid-free paper. When it is available, we choose paper that has been manufactured by environmentally responsible processes. These may include using trees grown in sustainable forests, incorporating recycled paper, minimizing chlorine in bleaching, or recycling the energy produced at the paper mill.

Library of Congress Cataloging-in-Publication Data
Names: Shallenberger, Rob, author. | Shallenberger, Steve, author.
Title: Do what matters most : lead a life by design, not by default / Rob Shallenberger & Steve Shallenberger.
Description: Second edition. | Oakland, CA : Berrett-Koehler Publishers, Inc., [2025] | ncludes bibliographical references and index.
Identifiers: LCCN 2024026779 (print) | LCCN 2024026780 (ebook) | ISBN 9798890570512 (paperback) | ISBN 9798890570529 (pdf) | ISBN 9798890570536 (epub)
Subjects: LCSH: Time management. | Goal (Psychology) | Performance. | Success in business.
Classification: LCC HD69.T54 S53 2025 (print) | LCC HD69.T54 (ebook) | DDC 650.1/1—dc23/eng/20241010
LC record available at https://lccn.loc.gov/2024026779
LC ebook record available at https://lccn.loc.gov/2024026780

Second Edition
32 31 30 29 28 27 26 25 24 10 9 8 7 6 5 4 3 2 1

Book interior design and production: Happenstance Type-O-Rama
Cover design: Irene Morris/Ashley Ingram

This book is dedicated to the many friends and family members who have deeply influenced our lives, especially Roxanne and Tonya. In addition, it is dedicated to each of Steve's children—David, Steven, Tommy, Daniel, and Anne (and their amazing spouses)—and Rob's children—Robbie, Bella, Lana, and Clara.

CONTENTS

PREFACE

A common thread that binds many of us together is the desire to make a difference, find joy in life, have meaningful relationships, be healthy, and feel productive professionally. Whether it's productivity in the office, relationships, or personal well-being, people are searching for a way to stay ahead of the curve and do what matters most. The challenge is that most people simply do not have a process or a place to start and instead are left feeling frustrated.

When it comes to time management and productivity, most organizations and leaders are thirsting for a solution that will help them prioritize their time and do what matters most. People are often asked to do more with less, which can affect their ability to sleep, exercise, maintain quality relationships, and show up in the workplace. Leaders strive to figure out how to improve results but often aren't sure what else to try.

Our research of thousands of people from more than 108 organizations found that 68 percent felt their number one challenge was prioritizing their time. At the same time, 80 percent didn't feel they had an effective planning process or program to stay on top of it all and prioritize what mattered most.

Based on a clear need for something to help close that gap, we have invested decades of research to develop a simple yet powerful program to help people take control of their busy lives and schedules. In this book, we'll share a program and accompanying tools to help you develop three specific habits that will increase productivity by at least 30 to 50 percent while at the same time reducing stress. This translates into teams who get things done on time or ahead of schedule, are better contributors, and are more actively engaged. For you personally, it translates into improved health, more fulfilling relationships, increased happiness, and, most importantly, a sense of control and balance in your life.

The three high-performance habits are to develop a written personal vision, set roles and goals for this year, and consistently do pre-week planning. While terms like *vision*, *goals*, and *pre-week planning* will certainly sound familiar, 96 percent of people who go through our training have never seen them presented in this way, so it's an entirely new approach to leading their lives. Despite the familiarity of these terms, only 2 percent of people have a written personal vision, less than 10 percent have written personal and professional goals, and 80 percent don't feel they have a process to plan their weeks effectively. So, for as much as these concepts are talked about, there remains a big gap in practice, and most people are still looking for a program that works for them.

In this second edition, we'll share new research related to health, productivity, relationships, and their impact on our lives. Additionally, we'll introduce new and powerful tools we've developed to help people implement these habits, such as the circle of peace and balance and the digital planner for Chrome and Outlook.

One thing you'll quickly notice about *Do What Matters Most* is that it applies to everyone. We train private, public, and government organizations worldwide and have seen firsthand how this program has impacted people's personal and professional lives. From the CEO to the frontline employee, from the stay-at-home parent to the college student, people from every walk of life experience massive improvements when they focus on these three habits. This is not another flavor of the month; rather, this program becomes part of a team culture and a person's habits for the rest of their lives. We have taken years of training and compiled it in this book so that you have a simple place to start and know how to use the accompanying tools. It's common for teams to read *Do What Matters Most* together or for people to give a copy of the book to coworkers, friends, or family members because of its life-changing impact.

We invite you to test these powerful habits in your life and with the people you care most about. Part of that invitation includes reading the book from cover to cover because this program is designed to culminate in pre-week planning—the most important of the three habits. Ultimately, it's all about pre-week planning using the format described in later chapters.

So, after you finish the book, you can judge for yourself how impactful these habits are for you and how life-changing they can be for anyone—whether coworkers, friends, or family—who applies them.

INTRODUCTION

How to Accomplish 30 to 50 Percent More of What Matters to You

Amy was a rising star at American Express. Through the years, she excelled at her job and was promoted time and time again until she was in a senior director role. After some time in this position, she began to feel like something was missing in her life, but she wasn't quite sure what it was. She described it as simultaneously feeling that she had reached a plateau while also being overwhelmed by all the pressures and deadlines of her leadership role. She felt like she was no longer prioritizing what mattered most, and it seemed like she was always in reaction mode.

Amy was in her forties, so for a while, she brushed this feeling off as a normal development for her age. Her initial response was to work harder and put more effort into the seemingly endless list of projects at work. She thought that if she focused, worked harder, and finished some of the big projects, it would solve the problem. However, weeks turned into months, and nothing changed. Her attention would drift, and her energy would wane as each day wore on. Even though she worked harder, she felt less productive, and the pile of tasks didn't seem to get any smaller. Her supervisor, a senior leader, commented that it seemed like Amy's attitude and demeanor had shifted, as well as her productivity. This conversation with her boss only contributed to Amy's feelings of being overwhelmed and frustrated.

It wasn't just work, either. She felt like her relationships with her husband, daughter, and even some of her friends were slipping as well. She now understood what it meant to "bring work home" after a long day. She had a daughter who was born with a challenging disease, and Amy felt like she wasn't giving her daughter the time she deserved. As if the frustrations in her work and home life weren't enough, she also felt like she didn't have time to take care of herself. For example, she wasn't exercising or sleeping like she had in previous years.

Amy used words like *overwhelmed*, *frustrated*, and *in a rut* to describe her feelings.

How did this happen? How did this rising star get to a place where she felt this way? Maybe you can relate because you've felt like Amy at some point.

Amy wasn't the type of person to roll over and give up; she was committed to getting things back on track. However, she quickly discovered that there was a lot of noise in the world when it came to productivity, work–life balance, and time management. Amy read various books and listened to different podcasts looking for solutions. Through the subsequent months, she tried a lot of ideas that she picked up from multiple sources. She found advice like prioritizing tasks with ABC, time blocking, and identifying three big daily priorities and focusing on those first thing in the morning. These were all good tips, but none solved the fundamental problem: the most important things still weren't happening. Her life remained out of balance, and Amy could not escape this productivity rut. She was searching for a structured program and tools to help her be meaningfully productive, regain her life balance, and get her internal fire back.

It was at this point that we met Amy. She attended a Do What Matters Most keynote at a large training conference in Washington, DC. The keynote focused on what we call *the big three*:

1. Developing a written personal vision
2. Setting roles and goals
3. Consistently doing pre-week planning

After the keynote ended, Amy briskly walked toward the front of the room. It was apparent that she was on a mission to get to where we were standing. As she approached, she excitedly shook our hands and said, "This is it! I finally found what I've been looking for . . . a structured program that is simple, has the right tools, and will help me get my life back! I've read all kinds of things about vision, goals, and weekly planning, but I've never seen them presented this way."

She briefly explained her background and all that had happened that year, both personally and professionally. We were excited because she was excited. She had the right mindset; Amy only needed the skillset or the how-to. She promised to apply the new "program" and share her results the following month. We knew if she put in the effort to develop her vision, set her roles and goals, and be consistent with pre-week planning, it would significantly impact every aspect of her life.

True to her word, almost exactly a month later, Amy sent an email that said the following:

> I just wanted to let you know that vision, roles and goals, and pre-week planning really made a lasting impact on me. My boss, peers, and direct reports see a difference in me—that I am more positive and organized than I've been in a long time. Personally, I have lost 10 pounds this month, I've consistently exercised five times a week, and I've recommitted to all the relationships in my life (family, friends, and especially my husband and daughter). I'm finding hours in the day I never knew were there, and I've been so productive. The Do What Matters Most program changed my life!

Several months after she sent this email, we saw Amy again, and we could see the difference in her demeanor and attitude. Although we were excited to see this lasting change, we weren't surprised by this turnaround in her life. Once she had a framework and the right tools to help her implement the habits, Amy experienced a total transformation.

There are a lot of Amys in the world. At some point, we've all been there to one degree or another, perhaps even accepting our current situation as the new normal and doing nothing about it.

Like Amy, most people want to make a difference, be healthy, have meaningful relationships, and achieve peace and balance. The challenge is that most people don't have a place to start or know how to get there, which can be very frustrating.

Global events can magnify these feelings. For example, telecommuting while balancing childcare or trying to juggle everything on your plate while working remotely are all real and valid concerns.

One of the most common questions we hear from people is, "Where should I start or what should I do?" Our answer is that we believe real transformation requires both a mindset and a skillset. In other words, if a person or team wants to see a significant improvement, they must start with the right mindset, then apply the skillset. In Amy's case, she had the mindset—the desire and the discipline—so what she was searching for was the skillset. The fact that you're reading this book shows that you, like Amy, already have a growth mindset, and that's a big deal.

In this book, you'll also learn the same skillset as Amy, especially the habit of pre-week planning, as outlined in later chapters. One fascinating thing about this journey is that applying this new skillset substantially improves your current mindset and way of thinking; hence, not only does the mindset impact the development of the skillset, but the opposite is true as well.

Most people have heard a lot about vision, goals, and some form of weekly planning. Yet, as mentioned in the preface, 96 percent have never seen them presented this way, and it's a new approach to leading their lives. The specific approach and new tools shared in this second edition will bring all three areas together in a new and unique way that will start you on a life-changing journey, regardless of where you are today.

How This Book Came About

We have invested over 40 years researching great leaders and high performers—the top 10 percent in their respective fields. In that research, we found that there are 12 principles of highly successful people that you see over and over. These 12 principles are found in our other book, *Becoming Your Best: The 12 Principles of Highly Successful Leaders.*

After training hundreds of organizations focused on implementing the 12 principles, we saw that 3 principles always resonated deeply with people worldwide; not surprisingly, these were related to time management, productivity, and living a balanced life. Even though the Becoming Your Best training and book touched on these important topics, we knew there was much more to learn about them. It was obvious that people needed more than a few helpful time management tips or one more complex thing to add to their lives. That's why we set out to design a simple program and develop the accompanying tools so that people could take control of their lives and schedule their priorities. Thus began a new journey of research and development focused on helping people do what matters most.

Here are a few of the questions we wanted to answer as part of this research: What's the impact of health on someone's overall well-being? How about sleep and exercise? How do relationships impact someone's happiness? How many people have a written personal vision? How proficient are people at setting goals? Was their current goal-setting process working? If not, why? How do people prioritize their time and plan their weeks? Was their current approach to planning effective? When teams learned how to set goals and prioritize their time effectively, how did that impact their results? How did planning or the lack thereof affect people's stress levels, sleep, health, relationships, and overall well-being? How could individuals and teams consistently stay ahead of the curve and prioritize what matters most?

It's one thing to ask those questions in the abstract, but how about when they're applied to us personally? For example, how valuable is your health to you? How about your relationships: How important are those to you and your well-being? How important is it for you to feel accomplished professionally and that you're making a difference or having a positive impact? When we turn these questions inward, they become more powerful.

These types of questions and curiosity led us to take a deep dive into the areas of time management and productivity. With these types of questions at the forefront, we researched people in organizations from brand-new startups to widely recognized corporations. It was important to understand how these topics affected people worldwide, regardless of race, nationality, culture, or gender.

The research results clearly conveyed the need for something that would help people prioritize their time and do what matters most. When 68 percent of people cite their number one challenge as prioritizing their time, and 80 percent don't have a process they feel is working, that's a big gap.

After finalizing the research, we set about developing a simple approach people could use to regain control of their lives, find balance, and focus on the things that are important to them. So, while the original *Becoming Your Best* book touches on these topics, Do What Matters Most has become a well-tested program people can use to find balance and take control of their busy lives.

What makes this approach unique is that we'll invite you (and show you how) to identify the five to seven roles that matter most to you in your life. Then, you'll create a vision for each role, set one to four goals this year in each respective role, and develop the habit of pre-week planning through the lens of what matters most this week in each role. This holistic approach to leading your life is why so many people love this program.

As mentioned previously, the structured approach and how the big three habits come together is new for 96 percent of people. It's an approach that takes your life from the high-level view (your vision for each role) down to the weekly and daily level through pre-week planning. That's why you'll repeatedly hear us say *it's all about pre-week planning*. The first two habits of vision and goal setting involve *identifying* what matters most, and the third habit of pre-week planning involves *doing* what matters most. What's especially exciting is that 98 percent of people who consistently do pre-week planning indicate it substantially improves nearly every area of their lives!

Here's another way to think about these habits. Rob was a fighter pilot in the US Air Force for 11 years. During that time, he learned that the air force employs a strategic, operational, and tactical focus. The strategic focus applies at the command level. Operational plans are usually at the base level and focused on achieving the strategic intent. The tactical focus applies at the squadron level; in other words, it's where the rubber meets the road to achieve the operational and strategic goals. When you go through this book and learn how to develop these three habits, you'll be taking the same approach to your life:

1. Strategic focus: developing a written personal vision for each role
2. Operational focus: identifying one to four goals for each role this year
3. Tactical focus: doing pre-week planning to schedule your priorities at the weekly and daily level

This is why we refer to the process of building these three integral habits as developing your *flight plan* for life. The flight plan starts at the high level with the vision and culminates with the weekly habit of pre-week planning.

According to an old saying, "where your focus goes, your energy flows." As you go through this book and start on your vision, goals, and pre-week planning through the lens of your roles, you're determining your focus and where you want your energy to flow. This program is life-changing for nearly everyone who applies it (including ourselves), and the results are immeasurable.

The Guarantee

Our research shows that when you focus on the big three habits—vision, roles and goals, and (especially) pre-week planning—your productivity will increase by at least 30 to 50 percent. That means you'll accomplish an average of 800 to 1,000 additional priorities this year . . . all with less stress. Let's take a round number and assume you live for another 40 years; that's potentially an additional *40,000 plus* priorities you will accomplish because of Do What Matters Most. In every sense of the word, that would be life-changing!

Sometimes numbers on paper don't mean a lot, so how about if we make it personal? What if some of these priorities include spending time with family, scheduling a physical you've been postponing, taking care of your mental and physical health, finding ways to show up as a coworker or leader, taking a team member or client to lunch, or connecting with a friend you haven't talked with in years? All of these items culminate to represent your life, legacy, and impact.

Let's come back to this year. Even if challenges arise during the year (which they certainly will), you'll be better equipped to face them. Not only that, but you'll do so in a way that gives you power, resilience, and focus.

Life is more than time management; it's also energy management. Clayton, an operations manager who started using these habits about three years ago, captures this thought well: "This is more than just time management. It's a way of living that impacts every area of my life. Most time management tools focus on completing things or checking boxes (task-oriented). Do What

Matters Most is focused on the big picture; it's about intentionality and my priorities. It encompasses each aspect of my life and takes the whole picture of what I want to do and accomplish."

Imagine what could happen in your personal life and relationships when you find hours in the week you didn't even know were there. Picture being at your ideal fitness level. Think about what a great relationship with your partner, spouse, children, or other family members might look like. Imagine waking up in the morning, excited to face the day. Later in the book, we'll share the specific research around relationships, sleep, physical health, mental health, spiritual health, and having a purpose. You'll also see why those are important to you and how Do What Matters Most can directly impact each of those key areas of your personal life.

From the professional perspective, imagine what happens for a team when the average employee's productivity increases by 30 to 50 percent! Instead of running from fire to fire, team members can proactively prioritize their time and focus on the most important things. Instead of being task-saturated, team members communicate well, are responsive, and get things done on or ahead of schedule.

Developing these habits isn't a light switch that flips on and off, it's a journey. If you miss a week of pre-week planning, that's all right. Giving yourself grace is important. You won't be perfect; none of us are. Just thinking about your life through the lens of your various roles is a big jump for most people, and it only gets better the more you do it. Once you physically make the time to actually do pre-week planning, rather than just think about it, you'll see another jump in productivity, peace, and balance.

Later in this book, you'll see how this program took an "average" employee and helped him become the top producer on his team; how a mother of several young children was able to regain a sense of balance and purpose in her life; how a senior VP transformed who she was as a leader and reignited her team to achieve record results; how a manager went from always being "busy" and stressed to transforming his team and his home life; how a salesperson went from taking sick days because of their anxiety to significantly improving their sales results; and how a CEO who felt like she'd lost her edge regained her fire and passion.

These are only a few of the many examples you'll read about throughout the book. These experiences are from people who saw amazing results when they combined the right mindset with the skillset of the big three. Many of the stories in this book come from people who were already in a good place in life, but the big three helped them focus, do what mattered most, and get to an even better place. As you'll see, it doesn't matter what your starting point is today: going through this process is a transformational experience for anyone and everyone.

Take the Personal Productivity Assessment™

Before you read the rest of the book, we invite you to go to BYBAssessment.com and take a free Personal Productivity Assessment. This assessment will give you an objective score on how you're doing in different areas of your life. The goal is to improve your score and move the needle in a positive direction. The objective score translates into subjective results in your daily life.

After you take the assessment, print your results and put them in a place where you can return to them later. We invite you to retake the assessment after you've thought about your new vision and goals and spent a few weeks doing pre-week planning. When you apply what you learn in this book, you'll see considerable improvements in your personal and professional life. This assessment gives you a good starting point today.

Additional Resources to Help You Get Started

We've invested years developing and refining a paper planner as well as a digital planner for Chrome and Outlook. In this second edition, we'll show examples from the digital planner and teach you how to use it. These tools are intended to be a one-stop shop for your vision, goals, and pre-week planning. In most cases, the people who successfully stick with the big three habits are those who also use the tools. Having said that, if there's something else you would rather use for planning, that's fine. You could even grab a piece of paper and use it, if that's what you prefer. Developing the habits in Do What Matters Most does not require the use of our planners; they just make it a lot easier.

The whole idea behind our tools is to provide a solution that fits your needs. One tool isn't better than the other; it's simply about what works best for you. We offer three options:

- **The digital planner.** This is software you can add to your existing Google or Outlook calendar. For Google, you'll be adding an extension to your calendar. For Outlook, you'll need to download a plug-in to use within your existing calendar.

  Please follow the instructions for downloading the file, adding the extension, and activating the license. We'll explain how to use this planner later in the book.

  Note that this program is designed to be used with Google or Outlook calendars on your laptop or desktop computer. Although it will sync with your cell phone, it isn't an app.

- **The customized planner.** You can customize and build your planner to add whatever you want—meal planners, fitness trackers, habit builders, reminders, weekly reviews, and so on. You can also customize the cover so that it truly becomes *your* planner from front to back.
- **The Becoming Your Best planner.** This is your best option if you want a planner already built and ready to go. It has designated spaces for your vision and goals as well as for doing pre-week planning each week by role.

If you would like to invest in one of these planners, we encourage you to do so and have it accessible while reading this book. To choose the best one for you, scan the following QR code or visit DoWhatMattersMostPlanner.com.

Though these are paid tools and an investment in yourself, we want to reiterate that they are not required to apply the Do What Matters Most habits. They simply make it easier to develop and maintain these habits, and we want to do everything we can to help you succeed. Regardless of what you choose, we'll walk this journey shoulder to shoulder with you!

Let's Go!

We are excited for you and grateful you have made the time to read this book. Although you'll see many examples from team members, managers, and executives, the habits equally benefit stay-at-home parents, students, athletes, teenagers, and anyone else who applies them.

No matter your title, position, or stage in life, we are confident these habits will have a big impact.

So, let's get started and jump into the do what matters most mindset and skillset!

1

The Do What Matters Most Mindset and Skillset

As mentioned in the introduction, Rob was a fighter pilot for 11 years in the US Air Force. Years ago, Rob was flying an F-16 during a night training mission. He and his wingman were flying at 20,000 feet, and their two jets were about a mile apart. That evening seemed unusually dark, and the only visual frame of reference was the narrow field of view in Rob's night vision goggles. Everything seemed routine until Rob called for a hook turn to the left—a simultaneous 180-degree turn with both jets going in the same direction. As he called for the turn, a simulated threat popped up in the radar display over his right knee, distracting him. Instead of focusing on the turn and watching his wingman, he shifted his attention to the radar displaying the threat. So much was going on in the jet that he misprioritized what mattered most. That mistake almost cost him his life.

What Rob didn't realize was that when he started the 180-degree left-hand turn into his wingman (Rob was on the right side), his wingman mistakenly turned to the right. Without either of them realizing it, they crossed flight paths and missed each other by less than 50 feet, traveling at a combined speed of over 1,000 mph.

This hook turn was supposed to be a safe turn in the same direction in which they never got closer than a mile from each other. Yet so much was happening in the cockpit that Rob lost track of his priorities and nearly died. Unbeknownst to him, something similar was happening in his wingman's jet. The wingman had a light on in the cockpit that distracted him from his priorities, and he quit watching Rob, the flight lead. In the debrief, while they watched the tapes, both of them breathed a huge sigh of relief when they realized how close they had come to hitting each other.

Task saturation is an aviation term referring to when a pilot has so many things going on in the cockpit that they can no longer process everything. When task saturation creeps in, the pilot starts to *task shed* (drop things from their crosscheck or cockpit scan) and can quickly lose track of their priorities and what matters most. For example, in the cockpit, there are six primary instruments that a pilot should always be aware of, such as altitude and airspeed. Unfortunately, many pilots have crashed because they were task saturated, they misprioritized, and they lost track of their primary instruments—as Rob did that night.

Interestingly, it was not until the debrief that both Rob and his wingman realized how precarious their situation had been. During the hook turn, Rob and his wingman should have first ensured their flight path was clear rather than worrying about what was on the radar. Because they were both task saturated, which they didn't realize until the debrief, they misprioritized and focused on the wrong task at the wrong time.

Likewise, the busyness of life ebbs and flows. Although sometimes task saturation is extremely obvious, at other times, a person may not realize they are task saturated and may be lulled into a false sense of complacency. Task saturation is insidious, and the most dangerous form of it is when it is unrecognized—as it was with Rob and his wingman that night. Often, it's only when people step back to look at the situation (like Rob did in the debrief) that they realize how task saturated their lives have become. The point of this book is to give you a chance to step back and see yourself through a new and clear lens.

Looking at your own life, can you relate to that feeling of task saturation? Surely at some point in your life, you have felt the stress of having so many things coming at you but only a limited amount of time to accomplish them. When that happens, you likely know what we are talking about when we say that stress increases, productivity decreases, and communication (especially effective communication) goes out the window.

A common adage in many organizations is to *do more with less.* This approach is a perfect recipe for task saturation and everything that comes with it, such as lower productivity, higher turnover, and a decline in morale. Other feelings associated with task saturation include being overwhelmed, upset, frustrated, and perhaps unsure of what you should be doing. When a person is task saturated, it is easy to lose track of what matters most. In other words, when a person has too many demands competing for their time, it is common for their priorities to slip through the cracks. While it certainly manifests itself at work, the bigger toll often shows up in people's personal lives, which is why well-being and work–life balance have become such hot topics that have cost organizations huge amounts of money in lost time and productivity.

These kinds of prioritization and productivity challenges are becoming commonplace. It might be a stay-at-home team member who is burned out because they don't have a personal vision. Or, maybe it's a rising leader who has a solid mindset and habits but needs additional tools to prioritize their time and do what matters most.

Imagine a leader or team member who is task saturated like Rob was during the hook turn: How many of their "primary instruments" are likely to slip out of their crosscheck? This demanding environment is why the Do What Matters Most program and tools are so critical to helping people focus on their primary instruments or, in other words, what matters most.

Phrases you might hear others say (and maybe you have said them as well) as precursors to task saturation include "I really want to [fill in the blank], but I'm just too busy," or "I know I should do [fill in the blank], but I just don't have time." Sometimes, we wear that *busy badge* as a badge of honor, as if busyness equals productivity.

Examining your own life and the people around you, does busyness equal productivity? Certainly not if we're busy with the wrong things.

The truth is that when a person isn't focused on their priorities and what matters most, it can negatively impact their productivity, personal well-being, health, relationships, and even finances. In fact, being *busy* on the wrong tasks can do far more harm than good—we will explain more in Chapter 3.

There is a direct correlation between performance and productivity and someone's level of task saturation. When task saturation rises, performance almost always decreases. The most successful people know how to do what matters most and use their time on high-influence activities—those that produce the highest return for the time invested. That seems obvious, so why are time and productivity such enormous challenges for so many people? As mentioned in the introduction, we set out to answer that question, and that's how this program came about.

We have had the opportunity to see behind the curtains of hundreds of global organizations. A common denominator in almost every organization is that most people are busier than ever. Many feel like they are running from fire to fire or endlessly chasing the next shiny object, unable to catch it. Leaders have an enormous opportunity to help their people focus on what matters most and use their time on high-influence activities that contribute to the growth and well-being of the organization while also taking care of themselves and maintaining a high work–life balance. As a member of the executive team of Clif Bar said, "It wasn't until going through the Do What Matters Most program that I realized how connected my different roles were. I'd spent almost all my time in my professional role, which was taking a huge toll on other areas of my life. What was so unique about this approach is how it's packaged into a simple program. Once I learned how to use these tools, I realized there was a lot better way to lead my life and schedule my priorities."

At this point, one of the most common questions we get is, "Where should I start?" As we noted in the introduction, we believe the answer is that real transformation requires both a mindset *and* a skillset. In other words, if a person or team wants to see a significant improvement, they must start with the right mindset and follow it by applying the skillset.

The Do What Matters Most Mindset

Developing the do what matters most mindset is a journey, not a destination, and requires you to look internally.

It starts by asking yourself whether you have a *growth* or *fixed* mindset. Someone with a growth mindset is humble, willing to look at something differently, and hungry to learn. This mindset is characterized by thoughts such as, *What can I learn from this?* and *What's out there I'm not aware of that could help me improve?* In contrast, someone with a fixed mindset might think, *I'm fine the way I am* and not be open to seeing something from a new perspective. The fact that you're reading this book is a great indicator that you have a growth mindset.

The do what matters most mindset is described in one of our favorite quotes, attributed to St. Jerome:

Good, better, best. Never let it rest.
'Til your good is better, and your better is best.

It doesn't matter where you are today or what your starting point is. For a lot of people, life may already be good in many ways. For example, you may be considered a "good" manager, team member, partner, parent, or friend. However, the do what matters most mindset means honestly asking yourself, *What can I do to be a better, more productive leader or team member?* On the personal side, it might be asking, *What can I do to be a better parent, spouse, friend, son/daughter, or brother/sister?* Or, most importantly, maybe it's asking, *What can I do to take better care of my physical, mental, emotional, and spiritual health?* No matter your starting point, St. Jerome's quote invites you to consider taking one more step forward today to become a better version of yourself. In our experience, it's also safe to assume nearly everyone is going through a challenge most others aren't even aware of. So, whether life is good right now or you're going through a challenging time, if you continue reading with this growth mindset, you'll experience the life-changing impact of the skillset.

This growth mindset we're describing is also a shift away from reactionary living to proactive or intentional living. It is a willingness to make the time to schedule your priorities rather than letting your schedule dictate your every action. The do what matters most mindset shows the discipline to make the new skillset a part of your weekly habits. We like to define *discipline* as doing the right thing at the right time, regardless of how we feel about it.

At the same time, remember that it's important to give yourself grace rather than expect perfection, so that even if you miss a week of pre-week planning you'll still stay on this growth journey.

A great example to illustrate the mindset we're discussing came from a 92-year-old business owner in Kenya. During our workshop, he told the entire group, "My best is still ahead! I can't wait to finish my vision and goals and start doing pre-week planning!" Imagine the tone and culture this leader was setting throughout his organization. He clearly showed that he valued learning and growth, even though, statistically speaking, he may not have a lot of time left. He certainly communicated that he wasn't complacent or comfortable with where he was—even at 92 years old! This type of mindset is what leadership looks like, whether in your professional or personal life.

The Enemies of the Do What Matters Most Mindset

To develop and maintain a growth mindset, you need to be aware of several common enemies that might hinder you.

A mindset battle we have all faced to one degree or another is *complacency*. In the fighter pilot world, complacency is known as the silent killer, and it should be just as much of a concern for any individual or team as it is for a pilot. There is a long list of organizations that got too comfortable where they were and didn't pivot when they should have: Blockbuster, BlackBerry, and Kodak, to name just a few. Complacency is a close cousin to the fixed mindset. It can sometimes feel like being in cruise control. The complacent mindset is dangerous because it often closes the door to the idea that there might be a better way. For example, someone might say, *I don't need to worry about pre-week planning because my life is fine.*

Another enemy of the do what matters most mindset is what we label the *cynic* or the *skeptic*. Cynicism is a very natural emotion, and it serves as a filter or defensive barrier. Here's what we mean by a filter: What would your life be like if you believed everything you saw and heard every day? Chaos! The cynic or skeptic serves as a filter to wade through all the noise and block out what is not helpful. However, because the world is full of so much noise, many of us have let that natural emotion dominate our way of thinking. When skepticism becomes dominant, it can quickly become an enemy of the do what matters most mindset because you might brush something aside that otherwise could have changed your life.

We invite you to acknowledge that internal cynic or skeptic and then set it aside for just a few hours while you read this book and test the three habits. In other words, be open to testing the power of these habits in your life. In the spirit of *good, better, best*, see what impact these habits might have on your work and personal life.

The last enemy of the do what matters most mindset is *procrastination.* Procrastination—summed up by the words "I'll just do it later"—is one of the great enemies of success. It is insidious and can creep into any person or culture. We have all experienced it to a degree.

Organizational theorist and author Robert Anthony wisely said of procrastination, "Waiting is a trap. There will always be reasons to wait—the truth is, there are only two things in life: reasons and results, and reasons don't count!" In the book's conclusion, we'll share some tips and ideas on how to keep moving forward and eliminate procrastination.

It is critical that you remain vigilant about how complacency, cynicism, or procrastination could manifest in your personal life and within your team. The do what matters most mindset continually reminds you to keep your guard up to avoid these issues and enables you to maintain the growth mindset consistently. The skillset of a personal vision, roles and goals, and pre-week planning works to combat these mindset enemies.

Henry Mintzberg, a business management professor and author, wrote a classical article titled "The Manager's Job" in the August 1975 issue of the *Harvard Business Review.*[1] He captured the exact mindset we are describing when he said, "The manager is challenged to gain control of his or her own time by turning obligations into advantages and by turning those things he or she wishes to do into obligations. Free time is made, not found. Hoping to leave some time open for contemplations or general planning is tantamount to hoping that the pressures of the job will go away."

It is easy to blame a busy schedule or all the competing demands on our time for a lack of focus or productivity. However, adopting the do what matters most mindset shows a willingness to look at how things were done in the past and consider that there might be a better way. Once you are willing to see if there's a better way, the skillset becomes invaluable!

Stepping Outside Your Comfort Zone

Another way to think about the growth mindset and how it impacts your life is to consider the analogy of a rubber band. A rubber band is not designed to sit in a drawer. If it does, it loses its flexibility and becomes brittle. A rubber band is made to be stretched!

Likewise, as humans, we are meant to grow and be stretched. Sometimes, this takes us out of our comfort zone, but massive growth can happen when we step outside this zone.

We each choose to either lead a life by design or live a life by default. For example, our friend Dr. Mao Shing Ni is a 38th-generation healer and doctor of medicine (it's hard even to imagine counting back that many generations), and his father is currently 107 years old. Certainly, genetics and other factors play a role in that type of longevity, but rarely does someone live to be 107 without being intentional about their life choices. Hence, Dr. Mao and his family have led a life by design and experienced the benefits as a result. This type of intentionality in our life choices is part of being stretched and getting outside our comfort zones.

This stretch starts with a willingness to test the habits discussed throughout the book. When you do, they will positively impact your health, relationships, and well-being—even if you don't do them perfectly at first!

Carol Dweck, author of *Mindset: The New Psychology of Success*, said it well: "The passion for stretching yourself and sticking to it, even (or especially) when it's not going well, is the hallmark of the growth mindset."[2]

One of our certified trainers with the Florida Department of Transportation recently emphasized that this growth process is a journey and doesn't happen overnight. Some people jump right into pre-week planning, and it's an easy extension of what they're already doing. For others, it may take months to develop the habit fully. In other words, this program is not a pass-or-fail proposition.

Another person who recently completed a refresher course said:

> The first time going through the course, I didn't finish my vision and goals, and I only did pre-week planning for a couple of weeks. So, even though I wasn't applying the habits as I was taught, just the new thought process of looking at my life through the different roles was still life-changing. That alone was a great start.
>
> After the refresher course, I really started doing pre-week planning consistently. Even though thinking about my life through the lens of the different roles was great, actually doing pre-week planning consistently has become a total game-changer. I want other people to realize that it might take them some time to develop these habits, and everyone is on a different journey.

The point is that the process of stretching yourself and developing these habits differs for everyone and doesn't happen instantly for most people. Just thinking about your life through the lens of your various roles is a significant change for most people. That's why having the tools to develop the big three habits and the right mindset is a powerful recipe for success!

To illustrate the organizational perspective, the following is an example of what happens when a team has the right mindset and is willing to stretch.

A successful energy company in California had been working on these habits for years. One day, their sales team went through a half day of internal training focused on Do What Matters Most. This team averaged about 17 sales per day before the training, which was "good." At the end of the workshop, the trainer invited the team to set a new goal: averaging 34 sales per day. The new goal meant a big jump in sales and would require a different mindset and a new skillset to help the team schedule their priorities and shift their time to high-influence activities—what we call Q2 activities, which we will cover in Chapter 3.

You can probably guess the team's initial responses to the new goal. They said things like, "We've only hit 34 sales once before," and "I don't know, that's a huge jump." You can see in their responses how real the skeptic was in each of them. These are natural and common first responses for most of us. Despite their initial doubt and skepticism, however, the team members were good sports and set 34 as their new sales goal to average throughout the coming month. The next day—after being armed with a new mindset and applying the new skillset—the sales team had a record day. Their sales manager was ecstatic when she proudly shared with the trainer, "You'll never believe it. Today we just shattered our old record and hit 41 sales!"

A month later, this same manager wrote an email saying, "This has been so amazing. Can you guess what our sales average was this month? Thirty-four sales per day!" The team hit the exact goal they had set a month prior. This story repeats itself over and over when people and teams come with the right mindset and then apply the same skillset you will get in this book.

Do you think this sales team could ever go back to 17 sales a day and be satisfied? No. Once the mental bar (mindset) is reset, there is a new standard. This team shifted what their "normal" was, which yielded an additional $2.4 million in revenue for the company. More importantly, it meant more money in each sales rep's pockets and significantly higher job satisfaction.

This same type of mental shift can happen to you, whether it's in your professional results, health, relationships, finances, or general well-being. It's difficult to return once the bar is moved, because you've redefined your "normal"!

The Do What Matters Most Skillset

Having the right mindset is a great start, but it doesn't matter how good the mindset is without the right skillset. You wouldn't ask someone to perform heart surgery if they don't have the right skillset and training, regardless of how willing and motivated they might be.

The combination of the big three—a personal vision, roles and goals, and pre-week planning—makes up the skillset that will help you take control of your schedule and lead a life by design. When developing this skillset, you can step back and look at your life from the 30,000-foot view (vision) and then get specific, down to your weekly and daily actions (pre-week planning), where the rubber meets the road.

As mentioned in the preface, we researched thousands of people from more than 108 organizations, and 68 percent felt that prioritizing their time was their number one challenge. At the same time, 80 percent did not have a process for planning their weeks and doing what matters most. In addition, only 2 percent had a written personal vision, and less than 10 percent had both personal and professional written goals for the year.

Most organizations are thirsting for a program or approach that will help their people prioritize their time, do what matters most, and solve the task saturation problem. In fact, 84 percent of the people we researched felt that if they had a process to prioritize their time, it would have a big impact on their productivity.

Since 68 percent of people feel like prioritizing their time is their greatest challenge, and yet 80 percent don't have a solution, this is an area where the skillset can make a big difference, especially in terms of productivity, health, and work–life balance. We are confident that the big three will close this gap. Recall that 96 percent of people who go through the Do What Matters Most course indicate that organizing their lives through the lens of roles—especially when using the accompanying tools—is a new approach they'd never before considered. Like them, with the approach and tools you learn about in this book, you'll develop the big three habits and start on your own life-changing journey.

In his classic book *The Greatest Salesman in the World*, Og Mandino wisely said, "The only difference between those who have failed and those who have succeeded lies in the difference of their habits. Good habits are the key to all success. Bad habits are the unlocked door to failure. Thus, the first law I will obey, which precedeth all others is—I will form good habits."[3]

Vision, roles and goals, and pre-week planning are the skillset and habits that are strongly predictive of success. However, like anything, they take discipline and effort, which is the growth mindset part of the equation.

We like to use the term *performance average* to describe the current level of productivity across the different roles in our lives. Regardless of your starting point right now, when you implement these three high-performance habits (the skillset), they will have a tremendous impact on your mindset, and everything will seem to improve. Just like the change in the mindset of the sales team that went from averaging 17 sales to 34 sales, your performance average will increase in almost every area of your life. What this means for you is that you'll see the change in your health, relationships, and how you feel when you wake up each day.

When your performance average increases, you transform your mindset about what you are capable of both as a person and as a leader. In other words, once you raise your performance average, the bar is reset, and it isn't easy to go back. Applying the skillset raises the mindset, which is why the mindset and skillset are so closely tied together. Over weeks and months, they have a compounding effect. When you focus on one area, other areas also tend to improve. For example, when you increase your focus on your mental and physical health, sleep also tends to improve, which in turn improves your relationships. This focus on the skillset will be a compounding effect for good in your life.

What compounding results should you expect when you finish the book, apply the skillset, and increase your performance average?

- A purpose-driven life
- Improved productivity
- Significant improvement in workplace results
- Better health and work–life balance
- Higher-quality relationships
- Improved finances
- Peace of mind and a connection to your true, authentic self
- Reduced stress and greater peace
- Better leadership and team-player skills

Wrap Up

The fact that you are reading this book and going through this program already shows that you have a growth mindset. Your willingness to test the power of a personal vision, roles and goals, and pre-week planning will open doors of growth you may not have even known existed. Just like Amy in the introduction and the sales team that increased their average sales from 17 to 34, you'll be amazed by what is possible for you, both personally and professionally.

As you start this process, remember that it's a journey. Extend grace to yourself while at the same time focusing on the stretch. This type of thinking is the spirit of *good, better, best*, and the high-performer mindset. The combination of the high-performer mindset and this skillset will empower you to fend off task saturation, complacency, cynicism, and procrastination.

Before we discuss the Do What Matters Most program and the actual habits, we'll share our research, why it matters to an organization, and—even more importantly—why it matters to you.

REFLECTION QUESTIONS FOR THIS CHAPTER

1. What areas of your personal and professional life would you like to improve? What is your current mindset toward those areas?
2. As a team member or leader, what are some initial thoughts on how to be a better contributor or a more effective leader?
3. What's something you've wanted to do that would take you outside your comfort zone?
4. How would you define the growth mindset in your own words?

2

Why Doing What Matters Most Matters

If you were to place a value on your mental and physical health, what would it be? There's a saying that goes, "A person without health has one dream; a person with health has many dreams." If there's been a time in your life when you weren't in good health, you know exactly what that quote means. When someone is struggling with a health issue (anxiety, depression, sickness, disease, etc.), they have one dream: heal and get better. When they're in a healthy state, they can suddenly start dreaming about many other things.

As another example, think about the importance of your relationships. When you feel fulfilled in your relationships, whether with friends or family, you have significantly higher emotional bandwidth for your job because you can be physically and emotionally present when working. That also goes the other way: when you enjoy your work and feel like you add value, you can be present when doing things outside work and in your personal life.

Health, relationships, and personal well-being are obviously important to each of us. However, organizations should also pay attention to them. If you feel like you're sacrificing any of those for your profession, it's become easier than ever to find an alternative.

Earlier, we said we choose to either lead a life by design or live a life by default. Well, we can shift those words slightly to a leadership and organizational perspective and say you'll either have a culture by design or a culture by default. Great leaders create a culture by design and take care of their people. It starts by ensuring their people have the tools to succeed personally and professionally.

Predictors of Longevity

The research around health and well-being is fascinating. There's enough research on those topics to fill a library, so we'll cite one study and summarize the remainder of the studies we reviewed.

In an 85-year study involving more than 2,000 people, Harvard researchers Dr. Robert Waldinger and Dr. Marc Shulz found that good relationships are the strongest predictor of happiness and health.[1]

Combined findings from numerous other studies point to several additional factors and predictors of longevity. But when we talk about longevity, we feel it's helpful to live a longer life only if it's also a high-quality life. So, wouldn't it be great to work toward living a longer and a higher-quality life? Another way to describe this is aiming for a long *lifespan* and a long *healthspan*. That's exactly what the Do What Matters Most program is all about.

These are the additional predictors of longevity from various studies:

- Relationships or social connections
- Life purpose
- Healthy diet
- Sleep quality
- Regular exercise (including aerobic and anaerobic exercise)
- Healthy weight
- Not smoking
- Moderate or low alcohol consumption
- Brain stimulation

Most of these won't surprise you. It's not identifying the predictors that's hard; it's the *doing* that's the challenge for most people. As you look at your life and the people you know, how many prioritize these areas and consistently focus on them? For most people, at least one, if not several, longevity predictors could use more time and attention. This is why traditional to-do lists and sticky notes don't work very well; they're still a form of reactive living and don't lead to consistent lifestyle changes.

What you'll quickly notice about Do What Matters Most is that it gives people the process and tools to prioritize these areas of their lives consistently. In other words, this book and the associated tools will touch every one of these predictors of longevity.

About 100 franchise owners for Curves (a gym designed primarily for women) went through the Do What Matters Most course, and they all laughed when the trainer noted that 85 percent of New Year's resolutions are broken two weeks into the year. The owners confirmed their gyms are full for the first two weeks in January, and then, sure enough, they empty significantly. Did the equipment change? Did the workout programs change? What caused the lack of follow-through on so many New Year's resolutions?

Whether it's exercise or any of the other predictors from the previous list, most people would acknowledge that these are important things to do. But it's more than acknowledging them; it's about making time to actually do them consistently while maintaining balance in your life.

In our research and experience, the gap between knowing and doing for most people is the lack of a consistent planning process for scheduling their priorities week in and week out. If traditional time management worked, the numbers would be totally different. This is where pre-week planning and the other habits become game changers.

Deanna, a successful commercial real estate agent, recently shared that she had reached a point in her career where she felt stuck and didn't have the motivation she had when she was younger. Deanna was worried, especially at this stage in life, when she thought she could greatly contribute to her industry for another ten years. Deanna took the Do What Matters Most course, read the book, and invested in a planner. Two months later, she said, "This process of vision, roles and goals, and pre-week planning has literally changed my life and given me a focus and balance I never had. This process gave me new energy and purpose. Pre-week planning is a reflective process, allowing me to have a mental victory before the week even starts."

Deanna took the idea of leading a life by design rather than by default seriously, and it was life-changing. Like so many others, she didn't lack desire or intention; the missing piece of the puzzle was a structured approach to leading her life and prioritizing what mattered most. Indeed, going through Do What Matters Most brought focus and balance for Deanna because it positively impacted every one of those predictors of longevity. Like her, thousands of others have seen a similar positive impact, and so can you. This balanced focus is why doing what matters most really matters!

The Circle of Peace and Balance

Any team or organization is the sum of the individual team members. Therefore, when discussing things like productivity, health, relationships, and well-being, let's not start from a macro level but rather with your own life.

From this point forward, most of the book will focus on you as an individual rather than the entire team or organization.

Why? Because you are usually the only variable in the whole equation you can control. If you believe your happiness is due to forces in the external environment, then you're stuck. You're left with an assumption that isn't true—that the world is causing your feelings and challenges. In these cases, there is no way out because you can rarely do anything to change the external environment in appreciable ways. One variable you *can* control is what you choose to do with your time, energy, and thoughts. This decision will directly impact the balance in your life and, therefore, your peace. At some point, either you or someone you know was focusing heavily on one area of their life at the expense of another, which created an imbalance and probably took its toll.

Finding peace and balance is founded on building your inner strength and doing what matters most. What's awesome is watching the compounding effect of this balanced focus. In other words, when people focus on exercise, they also become more thoughtful about what they eat. When people eat well and exercise often, they usually start sleeping better, which positively impacts their relationships. As life balance improves, confidence, inner strength, and peace also improve. Hence, as mentioned in the previous chapter, this journey and process have a compounding effect.

So, with the focus on you, let's start by assessing your current situation and state of being. We call this quick assessment the *circle of peace and balance*.

To take this assessment, rate yourself in each area on a scale from 1 [poor] to 10 [outstanding], with 1 closest to the center and 10 on the outside of the circle. Once you rate yourself from the perspective of where you are today, connect the dots and assess your balance.

Figure 1 shows what a completed circle of peace and balance might look like.

Figure 1. A completed circle of peace and balance

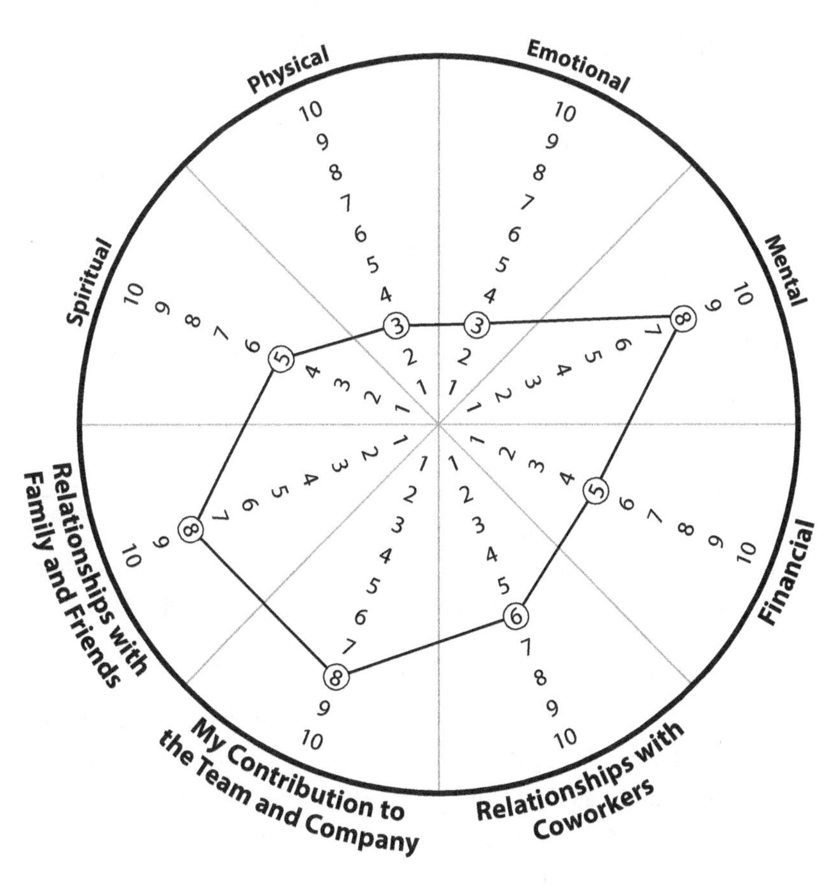

Before rating yourself, it's important to understand what each section means:

PHYSICAL: Exercise, weight, diet, blood pressure, cholesterol, annual physicals, check-ups, etc.

EMOTIONAL: Stress level, mood, sleep quality, meditation or yoga practice, mental health, and internal well-being

MENTAL: Reading, listening to audiobooks, practicing healthy thoughts, learning new skills, and investing in your mind—anything that keeps your mind sharp

FINANCIAL: Saving, investing, reducing debt, building financial knowledge, and keeping a budget

COWORKER RELATIONSHIPS: Relationships with coworkers, supervisors, and other team members

MY CONTRIBUTION TO THE TEAM: Engagement at work, new ideas, work performance, productivity, and overall contribution to the team

FAMILY AND FRIENDS RELATIONSHIPS: Relationships with your partner, children, extended family, and friends

SPIRITUAL: Internal connection to God, desire to leave the world a better place, and/or internal peace

Now that we've briefly reviewed each area, use the template in Figure 2 to rate yourself. After you've rated yourself in each category, connect the dots to assess your balance and current state of being.

The whole point of the circle of peace and balance is to get a snapshot of your life today. Then, use Do What Matters Most to do two things:

1. Increase the balance of your circle—in other words, your life.
2. Expand the circle outward. It doesn't help to be balanced if you're balanced at a 3. Regardless of where you are today, focus on balancing your circle and expanding it outward. For example, if you're a 4 in one area, a 6 in another, and an 8 in another, increase balance and then expand the balanced circle outward.

Figure 2. Template for the circle of peace and balance

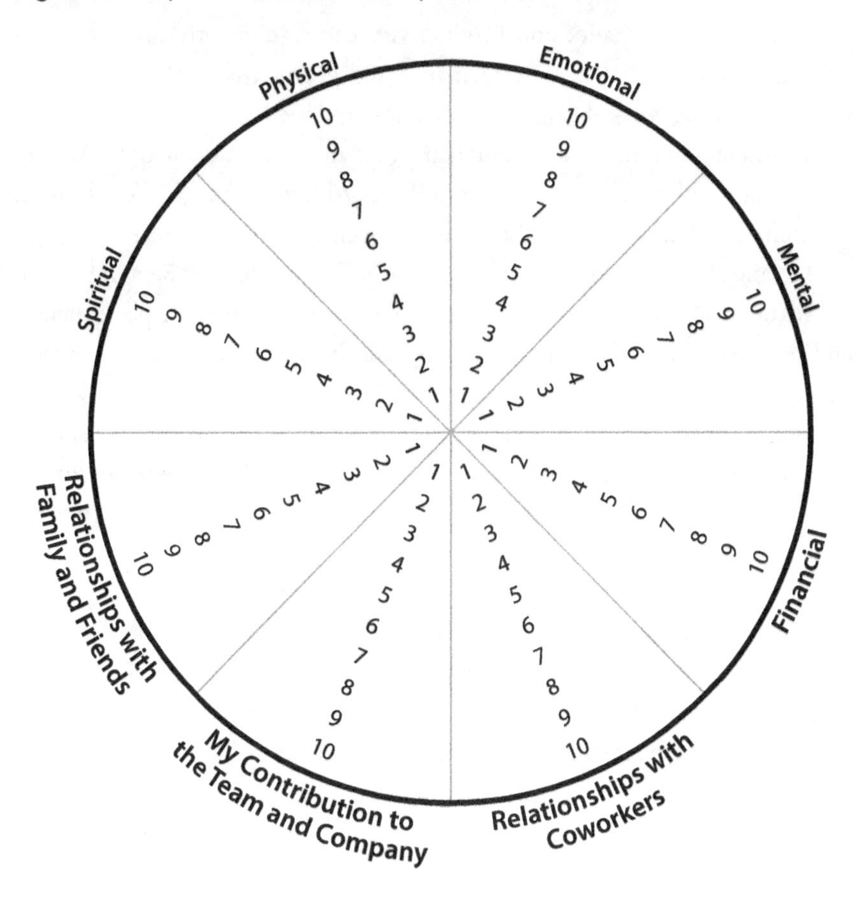

Some might say it's impossible to have balance, and it is without the right tools. Once you start applying the three habits and using the tools, you'll quickly see they expand your entire circle and positively impact every one of the predictors of longevity. As a result of this new focus, your chances of living a long and fulfilled life go up significantly. This balanced and holistic focus on yourself is why doing what matters most matters!

Performance and Productivity

Focusing on performance and productivity can significantly improve your circle of peace and balance. Performance and productivity affect every area of life, including work, health, relationships, and well-being.

Consider a hypothetical person named Adam. Like many people, Adam's been so busy with his career, family, and everything else that his focus on his health hasn't been what it could be. So, he decides, this is the year!

In January, Adam sets a goal to run a half-marathon by September 1st. If Adam wants to be successful, he needs to focus on both performance and productivity. It is both the *quantity* and *quality* of exercise that makes the difference. For instance, it isn't enough if Adam works out only once a week, even if it's a great workout. Likewise, if Adam works out several times a week, but the workouts are poor quality, he will not be ready for the half-marathon either. Adam must combine high-quality workouts (performance) with enough repetition (productivity) to achieve his goal.

As you can see, this focus on performance and productivity applies to your professional and personal goals. Adam won't magically be ready for the half-marathon without the proper focus and preparation. During his preparation, he will likely fight the same battles many fight—procrastination, chasing the next shiny object, or being "too busy." In Adam's case, his vision, goals, and pre-week planning will help him make time to train and prepare. For you, maybe it isn't a half-marathon; instead, perhaps you want to increase your focus on your health, mental and emotional well-being, job performance, or relationships.

From the organizational perspective, the best leaders want their teams to focus on high-impact activities and perform them as much as possible. The same thought process applies whether the team works in manufacturing, sales, marketing, HR, or elsewhere. For example, suppose you lead a group of technicians who service homes. You want those technicians to service as many homes as possible, delivering as close as possible to perfect service—high performance and high productivity. Isn't that much better than a technician with a 30 percent return rate to fix problems that should have been addressed on their first visit?

Everything we've discussed may seem obvious, but it's amazing how this area is ripe for improvement in so many organizations. When you look at your coworkers and others in your organization, what is your assessment of their performance and productivity? Focusing on performance and productivity is a great starting point for people who want to see a measurable impact.

The fastest way to simply yet powerfully get focused on high performance (quality) and productivity (quantity) is to develop the Do What Matters Most habits—especially the habit of pre-week planning.

The Do What Matters Most Research

When we started this time management and productivity research, the results were eye-opening, especially how Do What Matters Most impacted lives. When people participated in the program, they often used words like "life-changing." Once we saw the research results, it was easy to see how life-changing these habits really are.

Look at a few of these research findings on time, productivity, and well-being. While you read these, think about how they might relate to you (personally and professionally), your coworkers, friends, and family members:

- 68 percent of people feel their biggest challenge is prioritizing their time.
- 80 percent of people do not have a consistent planning process to prioritize their time.
- 84 percent of people feel they would be significantly more productive if they had a process or structured approach to help them prioritize their time.
- Only 2 percent of people have a written personal vision.
- Less than 10 percent of people have written personal and professional goals.
- A person is 90 percent more likely to accomplish something with a clearly written goal and plan.

- A person who consistently does pre-week planning will accomplish an average of 800 to 1,000 additional priorities in a year and experience a measurable decrease in stress.
- Pre-week planning increases productivity by at least 30 to 50 percent.
- 34 percent of US workers are actively engaged, meaning that only about one-third of employees are innovating better ways to do their jobs and contribute to the team. We realize other factors contribute to this statistic, but this is still an important data point regarding performance and productivity.[2]
- 12 percent of employees have called in sick because of job stress.[3]
- 53 percent of employees give the minimum effort required—and will quickly leave for even a slightly better offer.[4]
- Once you've been derailed from a task by an interruption, it takes an average of 23 minutes to get back on track.[5]
- 98 percent of people who finish their vision and goals, and consistently do pre-week planning as part of Do What Matters Most, indicate a significant improvement in their personal and professional lives (the circle of peace and balance).[6]

Of course, all these numbers are just a sampling of the revealing research. It's all too easy to look at statistics like these and dismiss them as meaningless because they're just numbers. But, when you look at them and realize these are people's lives, the statistics suddenly become personal and powerful. For example, when these numbers translate into rekindling a relationship with a son or daughter, successfully navigating a physical or mental health challenge, finally getting a good night's sleep for the first time in years, or finding joy in the workplace, suddenly they become real, and they're no longer just numbers.

In our experience, using Do What Matters Most to focus on performance and productivity gives people one of the most significant opportunities to see a real transformation in their lives.

Wrap Up

This program will improve every area of your circle of peace and balance, or in other words, your life. This focus on your personal and professional lives raises your *performance average*. For example, we found that someone with a significant personal issue will be about 40 percent less productive at work. By reverse logic, a person with a balance of success stories in their various roles will be 40 percent more productive in the workplace. The point is that you are a sum of your roles, and each is important to your overall success.

As you've already seen, it's common for people who go through Do What Matters Most to say they found time they never knew they had. You will feel the power that comes with a sense of direction and purpose. Task saturation and stress will both decrease while performance and productivity increase. You will take care of your physical and mental health and devote more quality time to the important people in your life. In short, we are confident that applying these three habits will support your journey to becoming happier and healthier and living a more fulfilled and purposeful life. We can confidently make that statement because we have seen it happen in our own lives, in people like Amy and Deanna, and in thousands of others.

REFLECTION QUESTIONS FOR THIS CHAPTER

1. Which area(s) of your circle of peace and balance would you like to improve?
2. How would it positively impact your life to focus on those areas and expand your circle?

3

Schedule Your Priorities

Dwight D. Eisenhower was a brilliant man in terms of productivity and organization. He was the 34th US president, one of only nine officers in the history of the US Army to become a five-star general, and the supreme allied commander who coordinated the D-Day invasion toward the end of World War II. He also developed what was originally called the *Eisenhower Matrix*.

Over the years, various people have used Eisenhower's matrix with their own spin, but its essence has always remained the same. We have taken the liberty of making a few adjustments to the original matrix; for this reason, we call it the Do What Matters Most matrix instead. While this matrix's organizational application is very helpful, as you look at it in Figure 3, consider how it also applies to your health, relationships, and personal well-being.

Figure 3. The Do What Matters Most matrix

	URGENT	NOT URGENT
IMPORTANT	**Q1** **DO IT!** High-stress, high-priority **EXAMPLES** Crises, emergency meetings, client concerns, pressing problems, deadlines, fires, emergencies	**Q2** **FOCUS** Low-stress, high-priority **EXAMPLES** Roles and goals, pre-week planning, weekly alignment meeting, relationship building, exercise, strategic planning, personal or team development
NOT IMPORTANT	**Q3** **MANAGE** Urgent, not important **EXAMPLES** Some email or mail, unnecessary meetings or reports, interruptions, unannounced calls or visits	**Q4** **ELIMINATE** Not urgent, not important **EXAMPLES** Some TV, surfing the internet, wasted time, mindless activities

As we describe each quadrant, see if you (and, if applicable, the people you work with) can relate to it based on your experiences:

Q1: DO IT! This is the high-stress, high-priority quadrant. These activities demand your time because they are generally *urgent and important.* This quadrant is reactive by nature and describes a person or team that is often putting out fires. We will all be in Q1 periodically, but it should be the exception rather than the norm. If a person or team lives in this quadrant, there will likely be higher turnover, stress, anger, and frustration. Some people thrive on the adrenaline of Q1. However, sustaining high performance and productivity over an extended period is difficult because of the burnout that often accompanies Q1. Leaders need to be extra vigilant about minimizing their time in Q1, *especially* when they put other people on their teams in Q1 because of their own lack of planning. For example, a manager constantly dropping high-priority tasks on their team is likely to inadvertently put their team into Q1, which will greatly impact performance and productivity.

Q2: FOCUS This is the low-stress, high-priority quadrant. The activities are *important but not urgent*. This quadrant is proactive by nature and is where most high performers live. This quadrant is about scheduling your priorities to focus on what matters most while minimizing the time spent in the other quadrants. An intentional focus on Q2 activities will make time for exercise, meditation, upcoming projects, relationships, planned rest or vacations, improving processes in the workplace, and so on. For someone who doesn't focus or plan effectively, many things that should be Q2 activities will become Q1 activities. In other words, without sufficient focus and planning, a task that should never have been a crisis can quickly become one. We have all experienced the feelings that come with procrastination. For example, if we procrastinate and don't do our Q2 preparation, the closer the important task's due date gets, the more our stress increases.

People with a vision and goals who develop the habit of pre-week planning will primarily be in Q2. The big three will help a person concentrate on what matters most, properly manage the other three quadrants, and focus on high performance and productivity.

Q3: MANAGE This is the *urgent, but not important* quadrant. Activities in this quadrant require action but do not generally contribute to your goals or constitute high-impact activities. People in this quadrant often focus on filler tasks such as sending emails, holding nonessential meetings, and creating unnecessary reports. This is a quadrant where a person can appear busy, but they're not really productive. For example, how many times have you sat in a meeting and asked yourself, "Why are we even here?" That might be a Q3-type event. The idea is to manage the meetings, emails, phone calls, text messages, reports, or projects by what quadrant they apply to. Move an item to Q1 or Q2, discard it, delegate it, skip the email, or automate the task. A person doesn't want to be in Q3 because activities in this quadrant aren't *important.*

Q4: ELIMINATE This is the quadrant that is not urgent or important. Q4 includes any activities that do not make good use of your time, support your vision, or help you in any way. Without intentional planning, many activities during the day end up being a waste of time, which is one reason why productivity and performance suffer. A good indicator of a Q4 task is if your reaction is, "Well, that was pointless."

You likely know someone who spends most of their time in each quadrant. Where do you spend a lot of your time? Where do you think your coworkers spend their time? How about your family members? Maybe you know someone who loves the thrill of the firefight, and it seems like they create chaos and fires so that they can put them out. That is a person who lives in Q1. Maybe you know someone who seems to skate by, doing the minimal amount of work required for their job. That is a Q3 or Q4 occupant, and it is often frustrating to work with them.

Our research indicates that the optimal high-performance and productivity balance for a person or team is to spend 20 to 25 percent of their time handling Q1 issues, 60 to 70 percent of their time focusing on Q2 activities, 5 to 15 percent of their time managing Q3 activities, and less than 5 percent in Q4 (it would be ideal if Q3 and Q4 were 0 percent, but that's not realistic). These numbers will vary somewhat by industry and job, but they hold true in most cases.

The same research shows that individuals and organizations that struggle and are far less productive spend 40 to 50 percent of their time (or more) in Q1, 15 to 20 percent of their time in Q2, 30 to 40 percent of their time in Q3, and 10 to 15 percent of their time in Q4.

Two powerful questions to consider are: How does being in each of these quadrants impact you and others? What feelings do you and others experience in each quadrant? Your answer to these questions will affect your desire to focus on a specific quadrant and the results from that focus. Both knowledge and emotion are big motivators!

You might remember Amy from the introduction. Focusing on the big three helped her move to Q2 and transform her life. Before her transformation, without realizing it, she had been spending way too much time—more than 70 percent of her day—in Q1 and Q3. But instead of living in Q1 or Q3, she learned how to prioritize what mattered most and when to *do* the Q1 items. The process of identifying her vision and goals for each role, as well as consistently doing pre-week planning, gave her an entirely new lens through which to lead her life.

After just one month of implementing these new habits, Amy was finally making time to be with her husband and special-needs daughter, which was critical for her own emotional needs. She was making time to exercise and take care of her own well-being. She focused on her team members and found ways to connect with them and motivate them. Her supervisor told Amy she had never seen her so productive and happy. Amy was leading her team with renewed vigor and a significantly improved attitude. Most importantly, she was actually excited going into the week now instead of feeling the dread she had grown accustomed to.

When Amy spent more than half of her time in Q1 and Q3, she continually reacted to the fire of the day and chased meaningless targets; each day, she was effectively "winging it." This took its toll on her circle of peace and balance and the predictors of longevity mentioned earlier. In other words, the life she was living wasn't sustainable.

Armed with a new mindset and skillset, Amy moved into Q2 and took control of her life by doing what mattered most. As a result, her performance and productivity increased, her stress decreased, she was a better leader on her team, and she had a renewed energy and outlook on life. Every area of her circle of peace and balance improved. Q1 emergencies still cropped up each week, but Amy was in a much better position to handle them, and because of her focus and planning, they became the exception rather than the norm.

Many people reading this can probably relate in one way or another. Most people have good intentions, and they want to do what matters most.

Whether it is increasing productivity at work, nurturing meaningful relationships, maintaining their health, or finding a purpose, people want to improve these critical areas of their lives. For most, it is just a matter of learning a process they can use consistently to schedule their priorities rather than prioritize their schedule. It is developing the ability to move past all the reactionary sticky notes and to-do lists to find the peace and confidence to *do what matters most* (Q2)!

Q2 Priorities

We want to share one final analogy to illustrate the importance of thinking about what matters most (Q2 and periodically Q1).

Imagine a classroom full of students with two large, empty glass aquariums at the front. Standing behind the two aquariums, facing the students, the teacher pours a box of ping-pong balls into the first aquarium until the balls are level with the top.

The teacher then asks the students, "Is the aquarium full?" The class responds, "Yes!"

Then, without saying a word, the teacher pulls out a box of small rocks and dumps them into the aquarium. The rocks find the small seams and holes between the ping-pong balls until they are also level with the top of the aquarium. The teacher again asks, "Is the aquarium full now?" The students respond hesitantly, "Yes?"

Again, without saying a word, the teacher lifts another box filled with sand and dumps it in the aquarium. Like the rocks, the sand filters through any tiny opening until it reaches the brim of the aquarium. The teacher then asks the class for a third time, "Is the aquarium full?" The not-so-confident response is, "Maybe?"

Finally, the teacher pulls out a large water pitcher and dumps it into the same aquarium. The water fills in any final gaps and ultimately reaches the rim. With a smile, the teacher again asks, "Is this aquarium full?" The students seem more confident now and yell, "Yes!" This time, the students are correct, as shown in Figure 4.

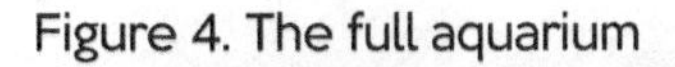

Figure 4. The full aquarium

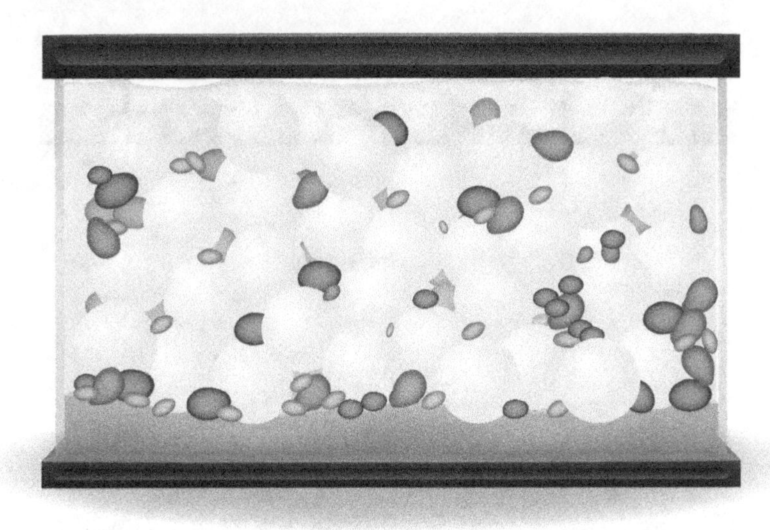

The teacher then moves to the other aquarium and pulls out a large water container. After dumping the water into the aquarium and filling it to the brim, the teacher asks the students, “Is this aquarium full?” The perplexed students are unsure how to respond, with some saying yes and others saying no.

The teacher then takes the same number of ping-pong balls as in the first aquarium and attempts to dump them into the second aquarium. As expected, the ping-pong balls float and fall out of the aquarium. Obviously, with the aquarium full of water, there is no room for the ping-pong balls, as shown in Figure 5.

The point of this example is to demonstrate what happens in our lives if we let the small things crowd out the big things or, in other words, when we let the things that matter the least crowd out the things that matter most. When the ping-pong balls were put in the aquarium first, there was still plenty of room for the small things (rocks, sand, and water). However, when the aquarium was filled with water, there was no room for the ping-pong balls. How often do you see something similar in your life or the lives of the people around you?

Figure 5. The aquarium full of water

This analogy applies to our personal and professional lives. This focus on your priorities is why vision, goals, and pre-week planning by role are so important. They keep you focused on what matters most, Q2 (the ping-pong balls), rather than being crowded out by the things that matter least.

Think about the things that matter most in your life. How important is your physical and mental health? How important is it to feel you add value professionally and have a purpose? What about sleep? Having enough money to live? How about your relationship with your spouse, child(ren), parents, friends, or other family members? These are what most people would consider their priorities, yet they're often the very things that slip through the cracks.

These habits will move you from any other quadrant and help you solidly stay in the high-performance, productive area of Q2. Even when a random fire or urgent item requires you to step into Q1, you'll know it's only temporary. When you have a vision and goals and understand the process of pre-week planning, you're in a much stronger position to do what matters most (schedule your priorities) and respond to any unexpected crisis or issue that pops up in Q1.

Wrap Up

The Do What Matters Most habits shift your focus to Q2 and raise your performance average. It's focusing on the priorities (ping-pong balls) rather than the minor things (pebbles, sand, and water).

The structure of Do What Matters Most—the three habits—and the accompanying tools work together to help you shift your focus to Q2 and schedule your priorities. They are designed to take you from the 30,000-foot view of your life (the vision) to where the rubber meets the road in the daily and weekly actions (pre-week planning).

That is why reading the next six chapters is essential. For example, setting your vision and goals without doing pre-week planning misses the biggest component of this program. Likewise, you could do pre-week planning alone, and it would be great—but it would be much better when done in the context of your vision and goals. Now that you've started this journey, it's critical that you go through each of the habits so you can see how they work in unison.

You'll notice that these chapters are paired. First, we discuss the respective habits and why they are important. Then, in the subsequent chapter, we share how to implement that habit in your life using the accompanying tools. For example, the next chapter is "The Power of a Personal Vision," and the chapter that follows it is "How to Develop a Personal Vision." First is the *why* and then comes the *how.*

So, let's get started on exploring why having a personal vision is habit #1!

REFLECTION QUESTIONS FOR THIS CHAPTER

1. What quadrant(s) do you spend most of your time in? How about the people around you?
2. What are your thoughts and feelings about each quadrant?
3. How would it feel for you and your team to be primarily in Q2?

4

The Power of a Personal Vision

What do people like the Wright brothers, Martin Luther King Jr., Amelia Earhart, Helen Keller, George Washington, Rosa Parks, Gandhi, and Harriet Tubman have in common? Although none of them were perfect, the common thread binding them all together is that they each had a vision.

When you read some of these names, you may think you'll never have that kind of impact on the world. It's important to understand that your personal vision doesn't have to change *the* world; it just has to change *your* world! Whether you're the CEO, a frontline team member, a stay-at-home parent, or a student, you can develop a written, personal vision that is meaningful to you.

Imagine how great it would feel to have a sense of purpose, clarity, and direction—to wake up excited to face the day. A clear vision provides that kind of fuel for your life.

We believe that your personal vision is the seed of your legacy. Imagine the massive trees that grow in the redwood forest. They can be up to 240 feet high and up to 15 feet in diameter, and every one of those giant trees started as a small seed. Likewise, most great accomplishments start with the seed of an idea.

Another way to look at your vision is from the perspective of your *dash.* If you've ever looked at the headstones in a cemetery, you've probably noticed there's a birth date and a death date listed. Between those two dates is a dash. It's interesting to look at that dash and wonder, *What were the relationships in that person's dash? What were the things they did during their dash? What stories or legacies are a part of their dash?* You're effectively writing your dash when you develop a vision for each of your roles. You're becoming intentional about what will be in your dash—and fortunately, your dash is still being written!

You have likely heard many times about creating a personal vision. However, our research has found that it is talked about much more than it's actually done. In fact, as we shared earlier, only 2 percent of the people we surveyed had a written personal vision. In this chapter and the next, we want to help you plant your seed and develop a compelling written vision that is meaningful to you.

When it comes to your health, relationships, profession, and the other areas of your circle of peace and balance, one of the most important things you can do is articulate your vision.

Imagine, from a professional perspective, how great it would be to have a team where each member is engaged and clear on their direction and purpose, has a desire and passion for being there, and has a personal vision that aligns with that of the team and organization. The process of developing a personal vision can be transformative both for the individual and for the entire team.

The unique approach to developing your vision shared in this chapter and the next will help you establish a well-rounded vision that will impact *all* aspects of your life!

The Wright Brothers

Before you start on your vision, let's return to the Wright brothers to see how their vision changed the course of history. Their vision gave them the direction, motivation, and encouragement to successfully design and fly the first aircraft—a feat that changed the world.

So, what was this vision? To successfully build and develop a flying machine!

Wilbur (1867–1912) and Orville Wright (1871–1948) were raised in Dayton, Ohio. One day, their father brought home a small toy helicopter made of wood. It had two rubber bands that, when twisted, turned a small propeller. Wilbur and Orville played with it until it broke; then, they made new copies of the toy themselves. They began to make additional toy helicopters and sell them to their friends. Thus, their newfound curiosity and innovation led them into the world of flight.

Years later, the Wright brothers opened their first bicycle shop. Initially, they sold and repaired bicycles, replacing spokes, fixing broken chains, and selling accessories. Then, in 1896, they began building their own bicycle brand. In August of that year, they first conceived the idea that man could fly. Keep in mind that they didn't even understand the principles of flight at this point. That August day was important because once they conceived the idea—the seed—it was the beginning of what ultimately became a powerful vision, one that guided their behavior, focus, learning, and time.

All of their bicycle experience helped the brothers in their investigations of flight. They used the technology they learned from their bicycle business—chains, sprockets, spoke wires, ball bearings, and wheel hubs—in their airplanes. Their thoughts on balancing and controlling their aircraft were also rooted in their bicycle background.

In 1900, they built their first machine designed to carry a pilot and chose Kitty Hawk, North Carolina, as a suitable testing ground. The area's strong, steady winds, open areas, and tall sand dunes were perfect for their experiments. When their initial aircraft design produced less lift than expected, the Wright brothers flew it as a kite and gathered more information that would enable them to rework their machines. They needed more practice, so they developed what they called a "wind tunnel" to help them simulate flight conditions while they worked to improve the design.

In 1902, using the wind tunnel, they discovered that to solve the control problems, they needed to add a rudder (see Figure 6). Realizing the importance of a rudder was one of the breakthroughs they needed to be able to fly successfully.

Figure 6. A diagram of the Wright Flyer

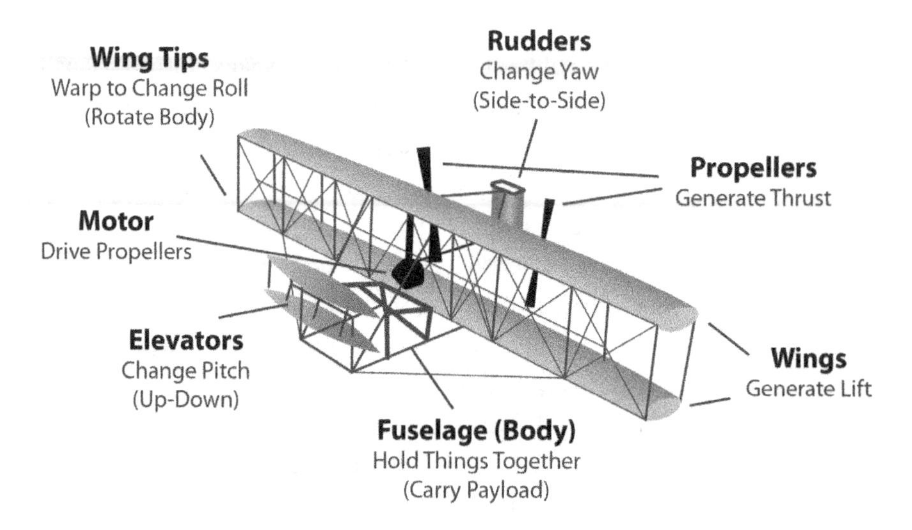

At Kill Devil Hills, on December 17, 1903, at 10:35 a.m., the Wright Flyer took off under its own power with Orville as the pilot (see Figure 7). It flew for 12 seconds and went about 100 feet. Orville and Wilbur took turns, making three more flights that morning. Wilbur was at the controls for the fourth and longest flight, traveling about 800 feet in 59 seconds. The Wright 1903 Flyer became the first powered, heavier-than-air machine to achieve controlled, sustained flight with a pilot aboard. Today, people can see this amazing flying invention at the Washington, DC, National Air and Space Museum.

In subsequent years, the Wright brothers continued to make modifications and improvements until they got to the point where they could repeatedly bank, turn, circle, and do figure eights with their flyers. On two occasions, their flights exceeded half an hour. Wilbur and Orville Wright, brilliant self-trained engineers, had overcome complex technical problems that had barred the way to mechanical flight for centuries.[1]

Imagine the power of that single vision and its impact on the next century!

Figure 7. First flight[2]

Naysayers likely told the brothers that what they were attempting could not be done. They had hundreds of setbacks, and like most innovators, they were likely tempted to quit at different points on their journey. But their vision was clear, and it provided them with a well of motivation and direction. It was this vision, coupled with their background and ingenuity, that made modern flight a reality.

Only after they conceived the *vision* to fly did they work on *how* to fly—first the vision, then the plan. It's the same with us: we first need to develop the vision, and then we can work on the how-to (goals and pre-week planning). The combination of mindset and skillset is what helps us turn the impossible into the possible.

The Wright brothers are a great example of the power of a vision. Remember, however, that your vision does not need to change *the* world like theirs did; it just needs to change *your* world!

The Influence of a Personal Vision

Nearly everyone agrees that it's essential to align a team around a clear vision. If that's the case, isn't it also important for each of us to have a vision that aligns our personal and professional lives?

In the Wright brothers example, you saw a vision that changed the world; now, let's consider some recent examples that illustrate how a personal vision can also change *your* world.

We had just finished leading a two-day conference in Johannesburg, South Africa. At the time, one participant, Jeff (who has since become a close friend), explained that he was leading an organization of approximately 2,000 people. It was evident from his demeanor and how he talked that Jeff genuinely cared about his team members and his organization's success.

During the conference, Jeff shared that he had endured several personal trials over the prior year, and they had tested him to the core. He was at a real low point in his personal life, and the issues he was dealing with personally were also taking a significant toll on his ability to lead his company effectively.

After the conference was over, the participants left—except Jeff. He walked up behind us while we took down the equipment and placed a pack of cigarettes on a nearby chair. We turned around, saw Jeff standing there with moist eyes, and asked him what was happening. Jeff responded, "For years, I have wanted to stop smoking cigarettes. I have smoked more than a pack a day, sometimes two, for a long time. Finally, it was when I developed my vision during this course that I realized cigarettes were no longer a part of my future. This pack [pointing to the partially empty pack of cigarettes] is the last pack of cigarettes I will ever use. My vision has changed!" Jeff had discovered that his internal *why* was now big enough to take on the challenge that had eluded him for years. We embraced in a big hug and congratulated him on his newfound vision and motivation.

Jeff related that he'd thought about quitting smoking for years, but he never made it past the phase of "good intentions." Going through Do What Matters Most and applying the same habits you're reading about now became a turning point in Jeff's life. His focus on his vision, roles and goals, and pre-week planning turned him around and helped him reconnect with a purpose. When you go through the same process of developing your vision, you will likely feel newfound clarity and strength as well.

What is powerful about having a vision is that we intuitively know when our life is either in or out of alignment with it. When our lives are out of alignment with our vision, it is our responsibility to get back into alignment—just like Jeff did on that day in Johannesburg.

A personal vision also changed Rob's life when he was 16 years old, shortly after his junior year in high school. That year was tough for him, and he felt lost and confused while trying to figure out life. His confidence was low, he didn't have any direction, and he certainly wasn't motivated. But everything changed on a warm July evening, when he and his brother Steven attended the Stadium of Fire in Provo, Utah—one of the largest Independence Day celebrations in the United States.

The festivities started with a fantastic fly-by of four F-16 fighter jets, which is always awesome. When the jets flew by, everyone felt the roar of the engines reverberate through their bodies. Rob and his brother watched in awe while the jets flew over in perfect formation. Rob and Steven looked at each other and agreed, "Someday, we're going to fly those jets over this stadium."

That July evening, focus and clarity came into Rob's life—the seed was planted, and the beginning of his vision was born!

From that point forward, Rob was committed to act on his vision to become a fighter pilot. A wayward and lost teenager now had a laser-like focus, and everything changed in his life. He went to work on the plan to achieve his vision. He knew he would need to graduate from high school, do well at the university level, and compete with a lot of cadets for a coveted pilot slot. At 17 years old, he earned his pilot's license after the required flight lessons, further fueling his internal flame to become a fighter pilot.

Years later, Rob and Steven became F-16 pilots in the United States Air Force. After years of preparation and hard work, they were much closer to making their vision from the Stadium of Fire a reality.

Fifteen years after sitting in the stadium as young teenagers, Rob and Steven applied to the Pentagon for approval to do the fly-by for the Stadium of Fire. Fortunately, the Pentagon approved their request. Although they had experienced some pretty amazing things during their fighter pilot careers, they knew this fly-by would be the proverbial icing on the cake.

On July 4, 2007, their vision became a reality. Rob and Steven, in a four-ship formation, opened the celebration and did the fly-by for the Stadium of Fire. Figure 8 shows a photo from Rob's jet, looking at Steven's jet on the far side of the formation.

After they flew over the stadium, the ground controller came over the radio and said, "Nice fly-by. Perfect timing. Congratulations, Shallenbergers!" The hair on their arms stood up, and both felt tears in their eyes. It was a special moment for everyone involved. Their entire family was in the stadium watching, many also with tears streaming down their cheeks.

After 15 years, their vision had become a reality! The seed of their personal vision, planted when they were teenagers, led to this memorable experience.

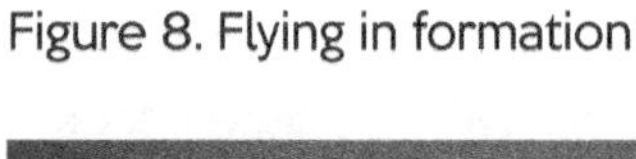

Figure 8. Flying in formation

No matter what your vision is, once you have it, it becomes the spark that ignites the fire inside you. This process of developing your vision is the process of *identifying* what matters most to you—that is, getting serious about your dash. Once you have your vision, you can develop your roles and goals and consistently do pre-week planning to accomplish them.

Create the Mental Reality Before the Physical Reality

One of the biggest challenges when we develop a vision is getting past the hurdle between our ears—our mindset. One of the most important things you can do in developing your vision is to let the creative ideas flow and not worry about all the potential constraints and roadblocks in your way.

You might compare the importance of the mindset to designing and building your dream home. Imagine the look and feel of the house. Envision yourself driving up to it, walking to the front door, and entering the home. Imagine looking in the main room and admiring every feature. In your dream home, you have had no constraints. You have been able to build whatever you want. Picture yourself looking at the woodwork, the landscaping, the beautiful kitchen, and the living room. What do you see?

Now, backtrack and consider what you need to build this home. At a minimum, you need money, property, and a plan like the one shown in Figure 9.

Would you build your home without a blueprint or plan? Of course not! Without a solid plan, the design may not meet the city's codes, you'll probably have costly overruns and miscommunications with contractors, and undoubtedly, the home will turn out differently than you had envisioned.

When you have a plan, you can see everything beforehand. You can see the result in your mind's eye before the house is even built. You can review the plans with your partner and family to be sure everyone agrees. Once you begin construction, the plan is a communication tool to ensure that everyone is aligned.

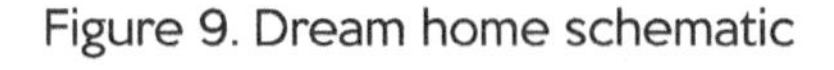
Figure 9. Dream home schematic

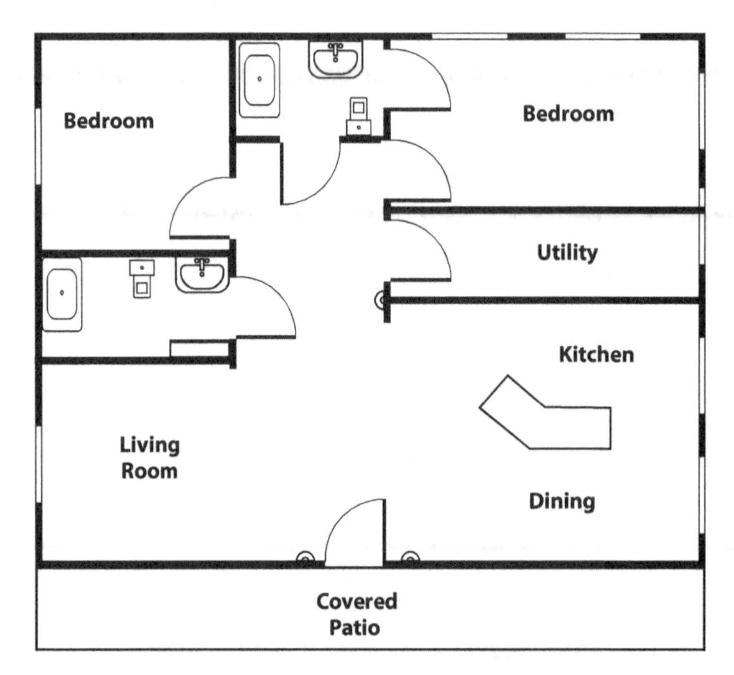

If you had only one shot at building your dream home, you would likely be meticulous about your plans. We only get one shot at life, so think about how important it is to lead a life by design.

When building your dream home, you use your imagination to create the thought, or mental picture, of the home. Then, you get to work on actually building and constructing it.

Your vision is about creating the mental reality before the physical reality. Once you dream it, you can achieve it. Once you have a clear mental picture, you become intently focused on it. Life's journey gets exciting when you can get up in the morning and know what you're working toward because you've already seen it in your mind's eye. Your personal vision will add direction, texture, light, color, imagination, music, richness, and amazement to your life.

A Clear Vision Can Transform Your Life

A vision has preceded almost every great accomplishment throughout history. Think of these famous visions:

- John F. Kennedy: Put a man on the moon.
- Rosa Parks: Equality for all.
- Elon Musk: Put people back into space, colonize the moon, go to Mars.
- Amelia Earhart: Be the first woman to fly solo across the Atlantic.
- Bill Gates: Have a computer in every home.

Their vision guided each one of these influential leaders. Imagine the tremendous power of an idea or dream—it can literally unleash magic in your life and organization. There are great rewards to periodically sitting back for a few minutes to pause and think. Successful leadership is about leading a life by *design* rather than living a life by *default*!

From a leadership perspective, leadership is also about bringing out the best in others. One of the best ways to lead your life and bring out the best in your team is to have your own inspiring personal vision and then help each person on your team develop theirs.

In his legacy book *Good to Great*, Jim Collins talks about getting your people in the right seats on the bus.[3] Think about how much easier it is to get a person in the right seat when you, as the leader, understand their talents, strengths, and *especially* their vision. Usually, a team member whose personal vision aligns with that of the team and organization is a better contributor and a higher performer.

Likewise, focusing on teams is what successful managers and leaders do. Imagine the power of a team in which each person has a written personal vision that inspires them and brings out their best. Even better is a team of people with inspiring personal visions; they've developed their roles and goals and consistently do pre-week planning. The odds are that this will be a high-performing team because its members are well versed in high-performance habits!

To take it a step further, if you are a parent, imagine helping your children develop a written vision that is meaningful to them. Leadership in the home is just as important, if not more important, than leadership in the workplace.

As an example, Steve and his wife, Roxanne, tried to provide their children with opportunities to see and learn new things. Steve and Roxanne believed that one of the serendipitous things in life is that in the right moment, providence would move on their behalf, and their children would each have a moment to capture a vision or dream that would profoundly influence their life.

Remember how Rob and Steven were inspired while sitting in the Stadium of Fire watching the F-16 fly-by? Another example of this type of inspiration was when Steve took his children to the county and state political conventions when they were young. One of his sons, David, still has photos he took with elected officials when he was just 12 years old. David was so impressed with public service that 30 years later, he got involved with politics at the state level. He, too, captured a vision of becoming a public servant, and years later, he is acting on that vision.

Similar things happened with Steve's other children. Each was exposed to ideas and formed a personal vision that deeply impacted their lives. Of course, none of the children is perfect, but what came from their personal visions has changed their lives as well as the lives of many others.

In one final example of leadership in the home, as part of her vision, Roxanne wanted each of her children to learn how to play the piano. As a result of her vision and hard work, all six children learned to do so. This tradition has continued with Steve and Roxanne's grandchildren, who are all playing or learning to play the piano. This type of legacy did not happen by accident. Roxanne's vision, leadership, motivation, and encouragement created it.

Taking someone's native interests, helping them plant the seeds, and encouraging them to cultivate those seeds is one of the greatest gifts you can give them. Whether you are in the workplace or the home, this is the essence of leadership!

Wrap Up

The famous lecturer and poet Ralph Waldo Emerson wisely said, "What lies behind you and what lies in front of you pales in comparison to what lies inside of you." A personal vision is exponentially more powerful when founded on character and correct principles. Each of our visions is about more than the destination; it is also about who we will become during the journey there.

Your personal vision, which lies inside of you, will change your world and all those around you as it deeply influences your life for good.

How much easier is it to get somewhere when you know the destination? Whether it's your health, relationships, work, or something else, it's important to create the mental reality before the physical reality. When you develop your vision, you'll determine what's important to you and what you want as part of your dash.

Developing a written personal vision is the first of the three habits. We like to say that developing your vision and goals is *identifying* what matters most. Pre-week planning is *doing* what matters most. First, identify *what* matters most with your vision and goals. Second, *do* what matters most with pre-week planning.

Once finished, your vision will become a wellspring of motivation and serve as your internal compass. It will guide you when you develop your goals and do pre-week planning.

Now, let's go over how to develop *your* personal vision!

REFLECTION QUESTIONS FOR THIS CHAPTER

1. How could having a written personal vision positively impact your life?
2. What role or area of your life would be most affected by having more direction and focus (a vision)?
3. Who else in your organization or family would benefit from developing a personal vision? How could you be the catalyst to help them?

5

How to Develop a Personal Vision

Now, it's time to start on your personal vision. To set the right expectations, we should clarify that you don't do this in just a few minutes. It will take a fair amount of thought and effort on your part. Whatever time you invest, it will be worth it. In fact, it might be one of the most important things you do this year. It also doesn't need to be perfect. Oftentimes it becomes a living thing that you adjust and make changes to over time. Just starting will be a powerful experience.

Ultimately, you'll want to have your vision in a place where you will see it often. That's why we suggest having your vision, goals, and a place to do pre-week planning in the same place—it becomes a one-stop shop. For most people, that will be in their paper planner or digital planner, as discussed in the introduction. If you haven't invested in a personal planner yet, you can flip back to the introduction and scan the QR code or visit DoWhatMattersMostPlanner.com to get yours now. If you don't want to use the tools we provide, grab a blank piece of paper, and you can use that as well.

For those using the physical planner, open to the Vision and Goals tab or the section that looks like Figure 10.

If you're using a blank piece of paper, see if you can make it match Figure 10.

For those using the digital planner, open your Chrome or Outlook calendar and click the Vision and Goals button. The digital template is shown in Figure 11.

Figure 10. The Vision and Goals section of the paper planner

My Personal Vision and Goals

"You will either lead a life by design or live a life by default!"

Role: Personal (Physical, Mental, Emotional, Spiritual)

Vision:

Goal(s):

Physical:

Mental:

Emotional:

Spiritual:

Role:

Vision:

Goal(s):

Figure 11. The Vision and Goals button in the digital planner

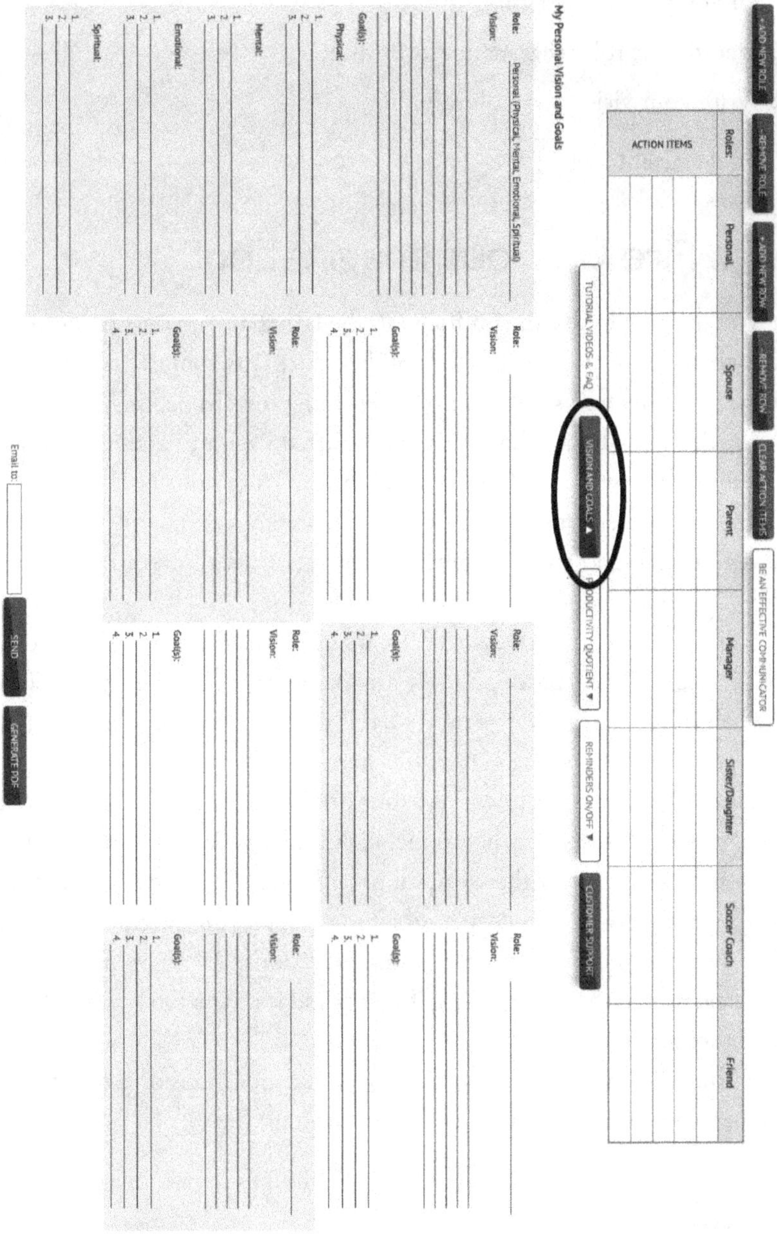

There are three steps to developing a vision that is meaningful and gives you direction:

1. Fire up your imagination!
2. Identify the roles that matter most to you.
3. Write your vision for each role.

Let's get started!

Step 1. Fire Up Your Imagination!

Just as you imagined your dream home in the last chapter, you first need to identify what you want your life to look like. Step 1 is about creating your mental reality or picture so you can start working toward making that your physical reality. It's about asking yourself what you want to include in your dash. Additionally, you can re-examine each area from your circle of peace and balance. In other words, what does a 10 look like for your physical, mental, emotional, and spiritual health? How about within your key relationships? In your career?

Thinking about your answers will fire up your imagination and get your mind in the right place. Although there are many other questions you could ask yourself to get started, we've narrowed it down to four simple ones that will help get the ideas flowing *before* you start on your vision.

People constantly tell us how these four preliminary questions were vital to helping them think about what to include in their visions. Invest as much time as you need to answer these questions *fully*. It's easy to stay at the surface, but we invite you to go deeper. For some people, this might mean you spend an hour or more on just these four questions. At a minimum, you should spend no less than 15 minutes; if you spend less, you likely could have put more thought into them.

To get started, write your answers to these four questions on a tablet or a piece of paper (it's far better than just thinking about them):

A. In the next 5 to 10 years, what are some things you want to do and/or accomplish?

B. Think of any mentors or people who have inspired you or positively influenced you (these can be people you know personally or historical figures). What traits do you admire about each of these people?

C. What would you like to improve in your job, home, or community?

D. How do you hope others will look back and describe you 50 years from today, whether you are alive or not (your dash)?

These four powerful questions help you think about what matters most. When you answer them, you will have started to design your home—or the mental reality of the best version of who you are becoming—*before* starting on your vision.

Each question does its part to get the creative juices flowing. For example, question B asks you to consider mentors or influencers who have inspired or positively impacted your life. Here are some answers others have listed about what they admire most about these people:

- They brought out the best in me because they believed in me!
- They had an uplifting and positive attitude.
- They had a sense of humor, knew how to laugh, and had fun.
- They sincerely listened to me when I needed a listening ear.
- They had hope and exercised faith.
- They took responsibility for their actions and owned everything that happened to them.
- They treated me with kindness and respect.

Can you sense how powerful this process is just by reading a few of these answers? Question B often causes a person to ask themselves, *If those are the traits and qualities I admire in others, shouldn't those be the traits and qualities I can focus on myself?*

Each question is reflective, making it important to consider before starting on your vision. Armed with your answers to these four questions, you'll be ready to start on your actual vision because you've put in the effort to identify what matters most to you.

Your vision is as much about *becoming* the ideal version of yourself as it is about accomplishing different things in life. It doesn't matter whether you are that person now; the power comes when you can articulate the person you want to be.

Step 2. Identify the Roles That Matter Most to You

We invite you to look at your life through the lens of the different roles that matter most to you. Throughout the day, you wear different hats based on where you are, what you are doing, and whom you're with, right? A few examples of roles are personal (physical, mental, emotional, spiritual), parent, professional title(s), spouse or partner, coach, church member, friend, brother or sister, and son or daughter.

When we think about roles in general, it is often easiest to think about our professional roles. But this step invites you to think about the other areas of your life that are equally or even more important. Dividing your life into your most important roles helps you maintain balance and think about what you can accomplish or do in each area. The focus on roles, along with the tools, is what makes this program so unique and different. This holistic approach to leading your life and focusing on your key roles supports your journey toward becoming the best version of yourself!

If you're using our paper or digital planner, you can see that each role has specific areas for your vision and goals. The rows labeled *Role* are where you write your most important roles. For now, you'll focus on the vision within each role. Ignore the areas where it talks about goals; that will be the focus of Chapters 6 and 7.

Several times throughout the book, you will read that your *personal* role is the most important role because it is *you* taking care of *yourself* first—physically, mentally, emotionally, and spiritually. You can only share your light when you have light to share. You can only draw water from the well when there is water in the well. Some people call this *self-care*. It doesn't matter what you call it: the bottom line is to take care of yourself, which is why there's such a heavy focus on your personal role. Interestingly, your personal role is probably the only role that's inward-facing (taking care of yourself), while most of your other roles will likely be outward-facing (showing up for others). You're much better positioned to show up in your other roles when you care for yourself first.

People frequently ask how many roles a person should have. Although there's no right or wrong answer to that question, the optimal number of roles is between five and seven. The number of roles you choose depends on your personality and circumstances, but you should leave room to increase or decrease the suggested number slightly. Remember, the whole point of roles is to create balance and focus on what matters most. You don't want too many roles because you only have so much time and capacity. For most people, the five-to-seven range is a good starting point.

Now that you've considered some of your roles, use the space in your planner to write your most important roles (the personal role is already listed in most planners). If you're using a blank piece of paper, write your roles and leave some space below or next to each to write your vision and goals. This is a draft for now, so don't worry about making it perfect. It's more important just to start.

Step 3. Write Your Vision for Each Role

Keep in mind your answers to the questions from Step 1. You started with those questions to get your mind in the right place and think about what matters most to you. Now, take some of your thoughts and ideas from those four thought-provoking questions and develop your vision for each role.

Ask yourself, *How would I describe the best version of myself in this role?* For example, how would you describe a transformational manager or leader? If you have children, how would you describe a great parent?

If you can aspire to be the best team member, parent, partner, friend, son or daughter, and so on, what will that look like by role? Again, first develop the mental reality of what your best looks like in each role so that you can create the physical reality.

It is important to clarify the difference between a vision and goals. Think of the vision as the end destination or desired outcome—it is the absolute best version of you in that role (your dash). It has an emotional component, and it guides your behavior and decision-making. The goals come later and are the specific milestones you'll focus on to make your vision a reality. You'll find it much easier to develop goals when you do so in the context of your vision. So, when you finalize your vision, it doesn't need to be specific or measurable; that comes with the goals. The most important part of your vision is that it drives your behavior and creates alignment for your actions in that role. For example, the vision in your personal role might be *I strive to prioritize my mind and body to be fit and healthy.* The goal might be to *Run a 5k by September 1st.*

When developing your vision, it is also essential that you use empowering words, such as *I choose*, *I strive*, *I am*, or *I will*, rather than weaker words, such as *someday*, *I hope*, or *to be*. Can you tell the difference between saying *I am a transformational leader who leads by example* versus *I hope to be a better leader*? When you write your vision and goals, words matter!

If you're like us, you probably appreciate examples because they often generate new ideas. Read the following examples of a vision by role, some personal and some professional, to get a better sense of what others have done:

Personal (yourself): I choose to live a balanced, healthy lifestyle. I strive to be in great physical shape and maintain a high level of spirituality. I am financially free with no debt or financial obligations.

Spouse/partner: I strive to be kind, compassionate, and help _______ feel like a 10. I validate their feelings and help them feel respected. I look for opportunities to compliment them, serve them, and be the partner of their dreams!

Friend: I surround myself with people who make me want to be a better person and who care about my success. I am a loyal, committed friend who is happy about others' success. I strive to create meaningful friendships and genuinely want to help, lift, and inspire when possible.

Parent: I exemplify what a kind and caring person looks like. I am the type of person I want my children to marry. I strive to be present with my children and continuously develop great memories. I invest the time and energy to help them see their potential, bring out their best, and make a difference in the world.

Sales manager: I am a transformational leader who knows each team member's story and invests in them. I set the tone to inspire each team member to give their best. I am the type of leader my team would still want to follow regardless of my title!

Again, your vision creates alignment and direction in a specific role. Intuitively, you'll be able to look at your vision for each role and *know* whether you are in alignment with it. If so, great. If not, then it is your responsibility to take action to get your life in harmony with your vision. Notice that most of these examples use "I" statements and focus on what you can control.

Look at Rob's actual vision in the role of husband, which is very similar to the spouse/partner role you just read:

> *I strive to be kind, compassionate, and help Tonya feel like a 10. I validate her feelings and help her feel respected. I am totally faithful in thought and action, and I look for opportunities to compliment her, serve her, and be the husband of her dreams!*

Is that how it always goes in their relationship? Of course not. But Rob knows when his actions and words are out of alignment with that vision. When he has said or done something that is out of alignment, it is his responsibility to fix it and get back to the vision. That vision also drives his goals and weekly actions from doing pre-week planning to scheduling date nights, sending kind notes, and so on. The whole point is that Rob's vision in the role of husband gives him a direction for his actions that is meaningful to him. That is what you should be able to say about your vision for each of your roles.

From a professional standpoint, wouldn't you want people on your team whose personal vision aligns with the team's vision? Also, wouldn't you want people on your team whose personal vision aligns with what they are doing in their role? In our experience, if a team member's vision is out of alignment with their role in the organization or with the organization's vision, they will be a mediocre contributor or performer at best. Conversely, high performers and high achievers often find that their vision aligns with their role and with the organization's vision. For this reason, everyone who goes through the Do What Matters Most training develops a vision for their professional role(s) or job title(s).

Here are a few more examples to help you generate additional ideas:

Personal: I strive to be organized and in Q2. I dive into new experiences with enthusiasm. I am always learning new and exciting things to keep me invigorated. I focus on being grounded, focused, and deeply connected with my inner self.

Artist: I bring color and beauty to the world by creating paintings that spark joy in others. I work hard to learn skills and techniques I can pass on to others. I spread joy through my paintings.

Student: I am a dedicated student who stays on top of homework and assignments. I work on having a positive attitude and being a great learner!

Here are a few more professional examples for various roles:

CEO: I lead by example and set the tone for our organization. I strive to help my team stay aligned, focused, and motivated to be the industry leader. I commit the time and resources necessary to develop people, create a high-performance culture, and align the strategy.

Manager: I aim to be a great leader contributing to an outstanding team. I am a key player who brings energy, enthusiasm, and a no-quit attitude to the team. I uplift the people I work with and help them become their best.

Sales rep: I do whatever it takes to ethically and legally close the deal. I have a no-quit attitude when I'm smiling and dialing. I strive to serve the customer and overdeliver in everything I do. I'm a team player because we ultimately win as a team.

IT team member: I help the rest of the team sleep well at night. I focus on being in Q2 to keep the email, servers, and website running smoothly. If there is an issue, I'm quick to respond and do it with a positive attitude.

Warehouse manager: Safety and quality are my highest priorities. I am a leader who clearly communicates expectations and leads the industry's safest, most efficient warehouse operations. I am engaged with my team members and continuously seek to improve our operations, with perfection as the standard.

Hopefully, these examples will help you get started. It is vital to articulate your mental reality so that you can go to work creating the physical reality. Remember, the vision is the destination or who you are striving to become in that role, and the goals (which come later) are the milestones to achieve the vision.

If you are in a position to do so, we invite you to pause here and invest whatever time is necessary to develop a draft of your vision. In the beginning, the most important thing is to write. Choose the roles that matter most to you, get your thoughts on paper or in the digital planner, and create the first draft of your vision. Then, you can sit back, read it, see how you feel, and decide whether it is your final vision or if you need to make some adjustments.

Remember, it doesn't have to be perfect—a point our trainers repeatedly emphasize. After you finish a rough draft of your written vision, you can run it through a litmus test. Once it passes the litmus test, odds are you have a great vision that creates alignment in your different roles.

The Litmus Test

After working on their vision, people often ask us, "How do I know I'm finished?"

For some people, the vision comes quickly and easily. For others, it's challenging and might require more time. Either way, it may be one of the most important things you do because you're defining your dash and desired legacy. The ultimate litmus test is to ask yourself two simple questions:

- Does your vision give you *direction* in each role?
- Is it *meaningful* to you?

If you can answer yes to those two questions, you've got it!

Your vision doesn't need to capture everything; it just needs to capture *what matters most* to you. The following are some reflective questions that might spark additional ideas for your vision (these are ancillary to the two key questions, so you don't need to answer yes to all of them):

- *Does my vision describe my physical shape, fitness, and desired health?*
- *Does it describe how I manage my money and my desired finances?*
- *Does it describe my emotional strength?*
- *Does it describe how I respond to anger, stress, or chaos?*
- *Does it describe how I treat others (my spouse, children, and coworkers)?*
- *Does it describe how I learn and gain knowledge?*
- *Does it describe what kind of listener and communicator I am?*
- *Does it describe my outlook on life?*
- *Does it describe my honesty and integrity—especially in the moment of choice?*
- *Does it describe how I take responsibility for my actions?*
- *Does it describe how I live in peace and balance?*
- *Does it describe what I do in the face of adversity, setbacks, and failure?*
- *Does it describe my faith?*
- *Does it describe my work ethic?*
- *Does it describe a state of being that moves me from where I am today?*

These are just a sampling of questions to help you determine whether there's anything else you might want to add, tweak, or delete from your vision. Remember, as long as your vision gives you direction and is meaningful to you, you've passed the litmus test! When you reach this point, you will have done what only 2 percent of people have done. Congratulations!

Hopefully, you feel a sense of accomplishment and a clear sense of purpose and direction. Crafting a vision can evoke a wide range of emotions because of how personal it is. It's normal to feel both excitement and maybe even nervousness because you're now like the rubber band example from Chapter 1—you are stretching yourself, and that's a good thing.

If you haven't finished your vision, we invite you to go to your calendar right now and block off some time to focus on developing and finalizing it. Ideally, you will do this within the next couple of days while it's fresh in your mind.

To help with accountability, you can write in the planned completion date here:

I will finish my personal vision by ________________[date].

As mentioned earlier, once you finalize your vision, we encourage you to put it where you will see it often. If you're using our planner (digital or paper), your vision and goals are in the same place you do pre-week planning. Staying aligned and focused will be easier because you see them every time you do pre-week planning. The point is to keep it in front of you; otherwise, out of sight, out of mind.

If you want to take it up a notch, consider memorizing your vision for each role. As a result of the memorization process, the vision will become deeply ingrained into your mind and heart. Imagine how great it will feel to have such a powerful internal compass!

Once you finish your vision, you can continue to build on this habit of staying centered on it. Some people find it helpful to create a vision board that complements their written vision. To create a vision board, simply put up pictures that represent your vision on a whiteboard or bulletin board, then hang it in a location where you'll see it often.

Another way to build on your written vision is to develop a lifetime bucket list. Create a list of things you would like to do in your lifetime. If you're in a relationship, you and your partner can do this individually and then come together to compare lists, look for overlaps, and prioritize those common items. Your bucket list can be part of your vision board or collocated with your written vision.

The vision board and bucket list are simple ways to continue building on your written vision. They give you added focus, direction, and energy.

However, the most important part of this process is developing your written personal vision by role. After all, the art is in the start. As Zig Ziglar said, "You don't have to be great to start, but you have to start to be great."[1] So, we invite you to start.

Congratulations on getting to this point. The fact that you are here is a big deal!

The Life-Changing Impact of Your Personal Vision

While you think about your vision, it can be helpful to hear stories from other people about how their vision affected their focus and productivity, both in the workplace and in their personal lives. Consider these testaments to the power of having a personal vision:

> *"Obstacles only become visible when we lose sight of the goal." This quote is one of my favorites and embodies the importance of a personal vision to me. Not only is my vision important, but it also drives me from my very core. My personal vision gives my life purpose, direction, and focus. It is sometimes easy to lose sight of the vision, to forget "what you care about," or get lost in the monotony of life. When this happens, I notice that I am not as happy or fulfilled; however, as soon as I recognize this, I go back to my vision to see how my actions align with my vision. Many times, I've slipped up, and it is not aligned, but just that realization is powerful because I can make course corrections to get back in line. My vision has changed my life. It's what gives me drive and purpose.*
>
> —ANNE S. P.

> *I recite my vision from memory almost every morning, and it really fires me up and ignites a deep passion within me to truly bring out my best to meet the day's challenges. My*

vision still brings a smile to my face and gives me a sense of purpose and drive that leaves me feeling full at the end of each day when I reflect upon it.

—MICHAEL L.

For me, my personal vision allows me to have greater happiness and peace instead of sadness, pain, confusion, or despair. What I learned recently was, I could rewrite my personal vision. This rewrite still had the core elements from the previous vision. However, because of many experiences and challenges, the rewriting of my personal vision has brought more happiness and allowed me to take on additional tasks and challenges with greater calm and peace. Having a personal and professional vision makes all the difference as I continue my journey in life. My personal vision is the foundation of doing what matters most each day.

—JULIE R.

Having a personal vision for the key roles in my life has had a powerful impact because these statements help me remember the kind of person I'm ultimately trying to become. Between having a busy work schedule, a family of eight, and other responsibilities, my weeks get hectic, and it is easy to lose focus. But when I sit down and review my personal vision for each role, as part of my pre-week planning, it centers me again on what I'm ultimately trying to accomplish in life. My personal vision has had a huge impact on the outcome of my life because it helps me to identify what really matters most. I strive to stay focused on my vision, overcome obstacles, and to "lift" myself and others to a better place as a result.

—JEFF D.

My personal vision is my guiding star, my compass, and a standard from which I live my life. It is the measuring rod for self-reflection and the foundation for all decisions. My son even put it visually into a coat of arms that reflects that vision . . . it is who I am.

—DAVID C. P.

Wrap Up

Your personal vision is the seed of your legacy, your dash, and your internal compass. It's who you want to become in each role. Ultimately, whatever story we tell ourselves, whatever mental picture we paint, will become our reality!

James Allen, a British writer and poet, wisely said, "The vision that you glorify in your mind, the ideal that you enthrone in your heart, this you will build your life by, and this you will become."[2]

The act of writing your vision is a powerful process, so we invite you to put in the time and effort to do it. It will be helpful if you actually block out time in your calendar to work on it until it is finished. For those in leadership roles, we invite you to help your team start on their written personal visions after you've completed your own. If you have children, and they are willing, you can also help them develop their visions.

Once you have a draft of your personal vision, it's time to move on to habit #2. The next two chapters focus on how to grow the seed and make your vision a reality by identifying specific targets for this year—roles and goals!

REFLECTION QUESTIONS FOR THIS CHAPTER

1. What was the experience of developing your personal vision like for you?
2. If you haven't finished your vision yet, when could you finish it in the next few days? Remember, it doesn't have to be perfect.
3. Where will you put your personal vision so that you can reference it each week as part of pre-week planning? Ideally, this will be your paper or digital planner.
4. Who else do you know—family, friends, or team members—who would benefit from going through this process to develop a written personal vision? Why would this process be helpful to them?

6

The Power of Roles and Goals

We have a friend—we'll call him Gary—who leads a well-known firm in the western United States. About five years ago, he attended a three-hour Do What Matters Most workshop with his Young Presidents Organization (YPO) chapter.

After finishing a draft of his vision and goals, Gary came up to us during the first break to relate how he had lost his edge over the past four years. He wasn't making clear decisions as he had in the past. He also felt his passion for the business had all but disappeared. He had seriously considered turning it over to his son.

However, he excitedly told us, he had experienced a complete change in mindset during the workshop. The act of starting on his vision and goals had reignited the flame. He was emotional when he commented, "I haven't felt this way for years. I feel focused and see a clear path forward." We told him what he was experiencing was just the beginning and invited him to finalize his vision and goals in the coming weeks. We also encouraged him to be consistent with the new habit of pre-week planning for the next three months and then call us with an update.

Three months later, Gary called us as promised. He was excited and spoke quickly, telling us, "The last three months have been some of the best of my life. I feel like I have my edge back, my mind is clear and focused, and my personal life is as good as it has ever been. The last three months have been some of my most productive months in years!" He shared that the first thing he had done after the workshop was to finish his vision, which kindled his internal flame. Developing his vision was the starting point to rediscovering his "why."

During that call, Gary explained that in conjunction with his vision, he had explicitly written down one goal during the workshop that made a huge impact. During the conference, we invited everyone to develop a specific reading goal for the year, because our studies have found a strong correlation between reading (or listening to audiobooks) and success. Gary set a goal that day to read an average of one personal growth book per month. After connecting the dots, he'd realized that he had quit reading about four years ago—the same time he started to lose his edge. He used to be an avid reader, but for some reason, he had stopped. During the workshop, he discovered that he wanted to start reading again.

Gary incorporated the Q2 activity of reading into his new goals, which drove him to pick up the habit again. He commented on how that one goal was responsible for a massive improvement in his motivation, leadership, and decision-making.

It might seem overly simple, but that's the whole point. How often do the seemingly simple yet important things in our lives slip through the cracks? How much easier was it for Gary to get back on track with reading once he developed the goal and did pre-week planning to make time for it?

There are many stories similar to Gary's—the truth is, at one time or another, we've all let important things slip out of our crosscheck. As we mentioned in earlier chapters, just thinking about your life through the lens of your different roles is a big starting point for most people. When you invest the time to finish your vision and goals and consistently do pre-week planning, this journey only gets better and better.

Like Gary, you may find that identifying your roles and goals is one of the most important things you do this year. It will give you focus, improve your circle of peace and balance, and positively impact every area of your life. Not only that, but imagine the professional benefit of every team member being focused on Q2 because they've identified what matters most in their roles and goals.

Getting Started

By the time you finish this chapter and the next, you'll have identified what matters most to you this year. In the spirit of getting the mindset right, we invite you to ask yourself these questions and put some thought into how you might answer them:

- *What would you like to accomplish this year in each role?*
- *What could you do this year to expand your circle of peace and balance personally and professionally?*
- *How will you specifically measure success this year in your different roles?*

These questions help you decide what matters most and where to direct your energy. Author and motivational speaker Les Brown once said, "If you set goals and go after them with all the determination you can muster, your gifts will take you places that will amaze you."[1]

This process will help you determine your priorities—in other words, where to focus your time and attention. Because we live in such a busy world, giving yourself time to think about your roles and goals will be a refreshing and powerful experience. You'll feel inspired, motivated, and peaceful when you finish this chapter and the next one. Both chapters are designed to help you through the process and write your goals in a way that sets you up for success. Developing your roles and goals is a decisive next step toward leading a life by design rather than by default. Remember, where your focus goes, your energy flows. So, in this chapter and the next, let's figure out where you want your focus to be.

Everyone reading this will have a different starting point. Many people say they've set professional goals at some point in their career, but they've never considered setting goals by role, especially outside of their professional ones.

You've certainly heard about goals your whole life, but you might remember from the introduction that only 10 percent of people have personal and professional written goals. When only 1 person in 10 has set both personal and professional goals, it's clear that for as much as people talk about goal setting, it's rarely being done. This usually isn't their fault; they've simply never been through the training and learned how to write goals in a way that's inspiring and sets them up for success. So, whether you've set goals your entire life or this is something completely new, you'll love the roles and goals process outlined in this chapter and the next.

Think back to the dream home analogy we shared in Chapter 4. Once you finish the home design, it can be built one brick at a time. Similarly, you'll pursue your vision one goal at a time—and reaching it may take weeks, months, years, or even a lifetime. Even though some goals may take longer to accomplish, when pursuing your vision, you'll likely feel an immediate shift in your motivation and productivity. Your vision provides direction and purpose, whereas the goals are the key milestones you strive for this year to make that vision a reality. The vision and goals come together harmoniously to create an inspired path forward. The process of developing your vision and goals is *identifying* what matters most; pre-week planning is *doing* what matters most. *Doing* pre-week planning is much easier when you've already *identified* your vision and goals.

On the professional side, we've surveyed and researched more than 108 organizations to learn more about how people and teams set goals. We also do pre- and post-assessments to measure results from before and after the Do What Matters Most training. Our research clearly shows that traditional goals are talked about often but rarely used in a way that improves results. We've found that the majority of people have never learned how to write goals effectively. Many organizations assume their employees know how to write goals, but as mentioned earlier, most people have never been through any type of training to learn this skillset—and it *is* a skillset! For example, there are certain words you should never use when writing goals, yet you see them all the time in professional goals (we'll cover this in the next chapter).

When goals are written and used correctly, leaders and team members can pursue them with a strong focus, significantly improving performance and productivity.

The other fascinating part of our research was discovering that people are 90 percent more likely to accomplish something if they have a well-written goal and plan. Imagine that: whether your focus is your health, a relationship, a revenue target, a sales goal, a production number, or any other important area, you're 90 percent more likely to accomplish something if you clearly write it as a goal (and look at it often)! However, that statistic applies *only* when you follow the goal-setting process and wording guidelines, as discussed in the next chapter.

Isn't it interesting that we're 90 percent more likely to accomplish something when we have a clearly written goal, yet only 10 percent of people do it? This gap is an excellent place for organizations to focus their attention. Investing in their people and training them in this skillset will almost always lead to a higher-performing team because team members will have identified what matters most and kept their focus in Q2.

Whether in a personal or professional context, it's important to understand that goals can be challenging for some people. One of the questions we asked people in our research is: *Why haven't you set goals in the past?* There was a wide range of responses, but these are some of the answers we repeatedly heard:

- They were never taught how to do so in their home, high school, university, or organization.
- The accountability that comes with a written goal can be scary, depending on the goal.
- Once written, goals become real, and the fear of failure sets in.
- Despite recognizing that goal setting is important, they've simply procrastinated and haven't made the time to sit down and do it.

Most of these concerns result from a lack of an actual process or structured approach—which isn't their fault. These are all easily addressed when someone follows the simple flow outlined in the next chapter.

When you align your goals with your vision, you identify the specific milestones for this year to make your vision a reality. You're getting intentional about your dash and how to improve your circle of peace and balance. This process will help you think about Q2 and how to prioritize what matters most. Your current starting point doesn't matter; this structured approach embraces the spirit of good, better, best to positively impact your health, relationships, work, and day-to-day focus.

John and Bella

Our friend John, an accountant with several children, has been successful in many ways and has always had a seemingly great life. However, we were talking one day, and he commented how he felt like he was in a lull. He admitted he had done well financially and accomplished many things he set out to do in life. Yet he felt as if he could accomplish more and do more than he currently was. We asked him about goals, and he responded, "I've never really set personal goals. I've thought about a lot of things I want, but I've never written personal goals." We briefly explained the process of developing roles and goals, and John decided to give it a shot. That year, he developed five specific goals—just one for each role.

One of his goals was to run a 5k in less than 30 minutes before July 30th. Another, for his role in the accounting firm, was related to achieving a financial performance target; this target was a big jump from where his performance had been the previous year. To his amazement, he accomplished all five of his goals by the end of the year. He said, "I would not have done a single one of these five things had it not been for my written goals and pre-week planning." This experience made him a believer in the power and focus of roles and goals.

The next year, John added more goals to each role, and he continued to see significant growth in each area of his life. It took him 40 years, but he finally sat down and identified the Q2 areas of focus that mattered most to him. As a result, he felt the power of leading a life by design and the intentionality that comes with roles and goals. And because he learned to write his goals as outlined in this book, his roles and goals didn't demand daily perfection but allowed for flexibility and grace in his days and weeks. By the end of the year, he had accomplished each one, and the cumulative effect was huge for him.

As you've seen, one of the frequent comments we get from people who follow our process is that roles and goals help them in *every* area of their lives. In addition to personal and professional benefits, people often tell us stories of what happened when they shared this program with their children, spouse, or friends. To illustrate how far-reaching roles and goals are, we will share another example—this time about Rob's daughter Bella.

Each December, Rob's kids sit down and develop their roles and goals for the upcoming year. Once they finish, Rob and his wife incentivize their kids with a fun gift or activity. One of their daughters, Bella, was 11 years old when she came up with the role of *author.* Rob was surprised because Bella had never really talked about being an author before. He asked her what goal she wanted to accomplish this year as an author and asked her to put some thought into it.

After thinking about it, Bella decided to write a children's book in the role of the author. So, together, they came up with the goal: *Write a children's book by December 20th.* Rob complimented her on setting a goal that would be fun and stretch her. A few months later, on a beautiful spring afternoon, they sat together on their lawn to review her goals. When they read that particular goal, she commented that she wasn't exactly sure how to go about it or where to start. So, they decided to write a book together as a fun father/daughter project.

They devised an action plan for *who* would do *what* by *when.* Bella would do certain tasks, such as developing the words, questions, and basic ideas for an illustration. Rob would find the illustrator and correspond back and forth to finalize the art.

They came up with the title *A–Z: The Best in You and Me.* The idea was to go through each letter in the alphabet and choose a catchy word associated with that letter—for example, A = Attitude, B = Beautiful, C = Courage, and so on. They also decided Bella would come up with a little quote associated with that word to put at the top of the page. At the bottom of each page, they would add a question to stimulate a meaningful conversation between the person reading and the child. Their vision was to create a book to help parents, grandparents, or teachers connect with the kids they were reading with. You can see an example in Figure 12 of "Beautiful." The question at the bottom of the page is *What are some beautiful things about you?*

Figure 12. A page from Bella's book

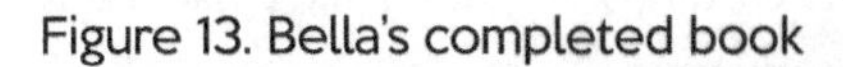
Figure 13. Bella's completed book

During the book's creation process, they encountered a few snags. For example, they had to go through 150 applications to choose the illustrator. The design of both Bella's book and the website dedicated to it had some hiccups, but Bella stuck with it—the goal kept her focused.

Eight months later, everything was complete. In mid-December, Rob and Bella rushed to finish the book in time to meet her goal. On December 20th, after a chaotic scramble to get the first copies printed, Rob and Bella stood on their back porch, holding the completed book in their hands (as shown in Figure 13).

Since then, people from all over the world have read Bella's book. She made enough money from its sales to pay for soccer and dance and save for college. More importantly, parents have shared stories with Bella about the great conversations they've had with their children while reading her book.

We share this story because it all started with the roles and goals process. Bella came up with the role of author and the accompanying goal to write a children's book by December 20th.

But what if she hadn't written that goal? *A–Z: The Best in You and Me* wouldn't exist. Bella wouldn't have met some of the people she has met, she wouldn't have made that money, and she certainly wouldn't have had some of the cool experiences she had along the journey.

The whole point is that if an 11-year-old can do it, anybody can do it!

Wrap Up

An old saying goes, "Action without planning is wishful thinking." Or, as the Cheshire Cat in Lewis Carroll's *Alice's Adventures in Wonderland* points out, "If you don't know where you are going, any road will get you there."[2]

Imagine how great it will feel to wake up with a clear focus on what's important to you—your health, relationships, profession, finances, and well-being. You will know what matters most and have a clear path forward to prioritize those areas (Q2) via pre-week planning.

Now imagine how great it will be to have your entire team focus on their roles and goals and what matters most professionally. Team members who go through this program find new ways to think outside the box and contribute to the team. They find better ways to do their jobs, serve customers, and improve the organization.

Our friend Jenny, from AstraZeneca, completed the Do What Matters Most program and saw such a dramatic improvement in her life that she decided to get certified along with some other coworkers and trainers. They've seen such a significant impact in their lives that the organization is rolling out Do What Matters Most globally as one of its four training programs this year. Once you go through the process, you'll likely feel the same desire to share this with the important people in your life. It only takes one person to be the catalyst for change in an organization or in the lives of those around them.

When you arm yourself with your vision and goals, you'll have a renewed focus on what matters most. You'll know where you're going and how to get there.

We hope you're looking forward to getting started on your roles and goals. We've spent years refining and developing this process to make it as simple and easy to follow as possible. In the next chapter, we'll walk you through the specific steps so that you're set up for success.

REFLECTION QUESTIONS FOR THIS CHAPTER

1. Thinking about your life, how could roles and goals be helpful to you?
2. What are your thoughts about goals after reading this chapter?
3. How could you help your family, friends, or coworkers develop their roles and goals (with a Q2 focus)? What would the impact be?

7

How to Develop Roles and Goals

As mentioned in the previous chapter, developing roles and goals helps you maintain balance and identify what matters most. That's the "why" behind goal setting, and now this chapter will explain the "how."

In Chapter 5, you learned how to develop a vision for each role. The vision is the strategic focus or internal compass that gives you direction and purpose for each role. The *roles and goals* are the operational focus and help you specifically identify your targets for this year. The goals are the specific milestones or focus areas toward realizing your vision. Although the vision is a feeling and an emotion, the goals are specific and measurable. At the organizational level, team members are invited to develop both annual *and* quarterly goals. But, for this book, we'll focus solely on you and your annual goals.

At some point during your career, you have likely been asked to develop professional goals for your position or department. Although that's a good start, roles and goals take it to another level. Nearly everyone has ideas about things they want to do and focus on to improve their health, relationships, job, and overall life. In this chapter, we invite you to take those good intentions you've thought about for years and turn them into specific goals in their respective roles. It's amazing how, when you finish your vision and goals, your environment seems to collaborate to help things come together in ways they never have before.

Before we get started on your goals, let's make sure you're set up and ready to go. If you invested in a planner and have it nearby, please open it to the Vision and Goals section, which should look similar to Figure 14.

Figure 14. The Vision and Goals section of the paper planner

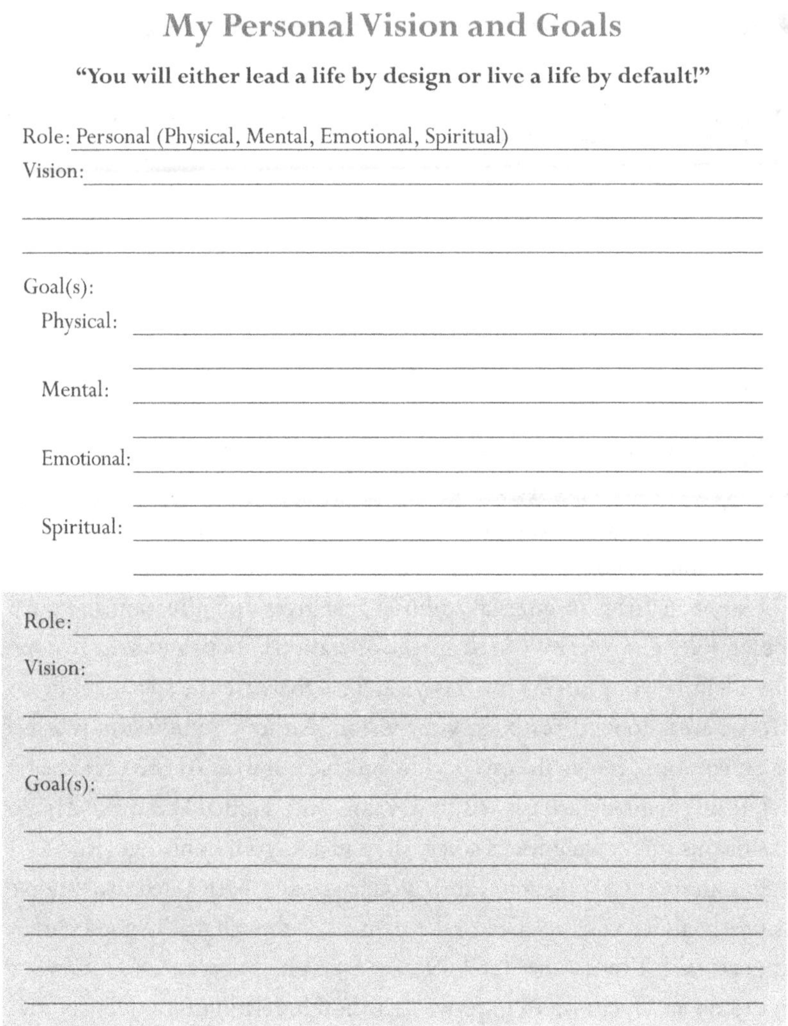

My Personal Vision and Goals

"You will either lead a life by design or live a life by default!"

Role: Personal (Physical, Mental, Emotional, Spiritual)

Vision:

Goal(s):

Physical:

Mental:

Emotional:

Spiritual:

Role:

Vision:

Goal(s):

If you're using the digital planner for Chrome or Outlook, open it and keep it in front of you while you read this chapter. Just as you did when setting your vision earlier, click the Vision and Goals button. You should see a drop-down section where you'll add goals for each role (as shown in Figure 15).

Figure 15. The Vision and Goals button in the digital planner

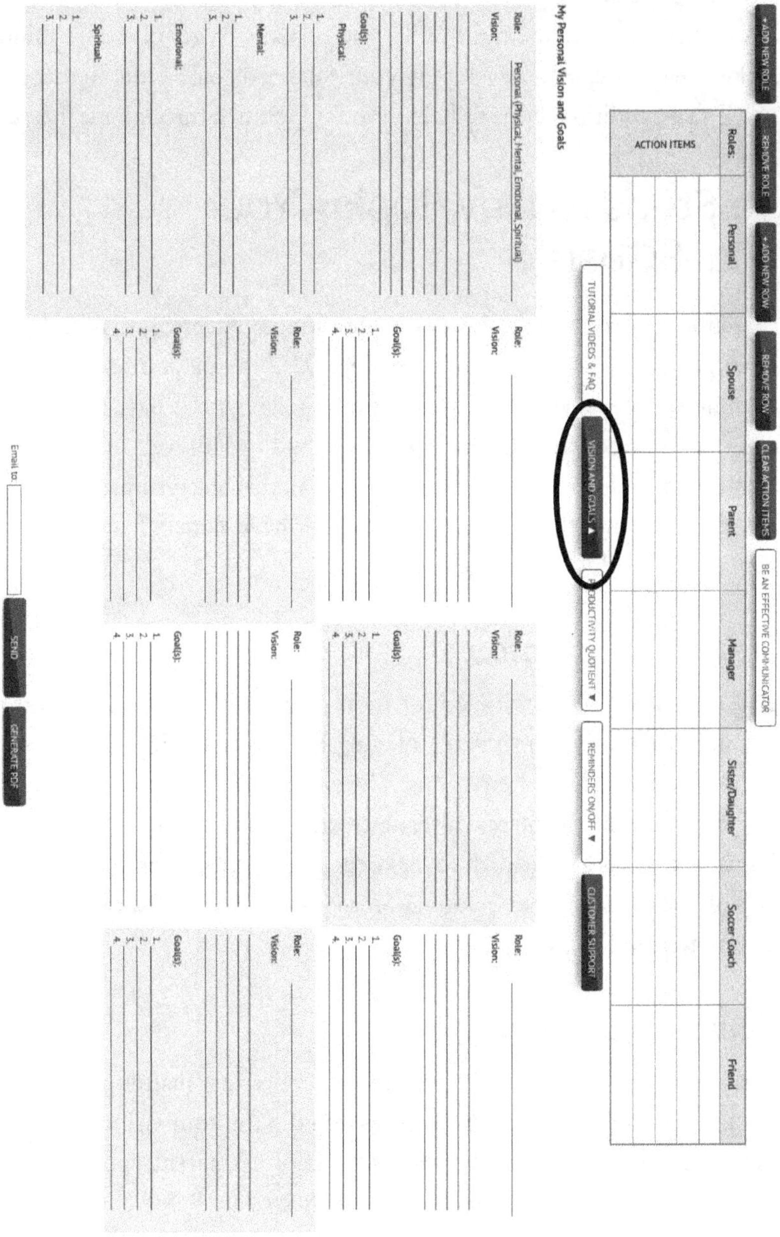

If you haven't invested in one of our planners, grab the same piece of paper you used for your vision, and make sure there's space next to or under your vision in each role.

Now that you have the right tools, you're ready to go. Next, we'll introduce the five key steps for developing your roles and goals. Later in this chapter, we'll share additional tips to help you stay on track throughout the year.

Five Steps to Developing Your Annual Goals

This section describes the five steps to developing effective roles and goals. This simple process will help you develop Q2 thinking and focus on what matters most. When you have well-written goals, you'll have focal points to improve your health, relationships, work, and overall well-being. Consequently, your circle of peace and balance will almost always improve significantly. By following these five steps, you will have done what less than 10 percent of people do. So, let's get started!

1. Review your vision.

Your goals should align with your vision. Thus, rather than focus on the problem, in this step you shift the playing field to the vision. The problem can be a negative vortex of emotions. The vision is filled with hope, motivation, and direction; it is the purpose, destination, or who you're becoming in each role. The goals are the path to make the vision a reality. When your goals align with your vision, they're much more powerful and meaningful than if they were to stand alone.

2. Identify your roles.

Just as you did with your vision, identify the roles that matter most to you. In most cases, you'll use the same roles as you did for your vision. For example, some of your roles might include leader, sales rep, parent, spouse/partner, friend, son/daughter, church member, or brother/sister. Remember, your personal role is your most important one.

We divide the personal role—and only the personal role—into four separate subcategories—all related to your individual well-being: physical, mental, emotional, and spiritual. *Physical* involves taking care of your body; *mental* is developing your mind and keeping it sharp; *emotional* is taking care of your internal feelings of stress and well-being; and *spiritual* is often about your connection to divinity or internal peace. Another way to look at these categories is to connect them to your heart, mind, body, and soul. It is essential to think about how you will take care of yourself in each area and form those thoughts into a goal. For example, Gary's reading goal from Chapter 6 was in his personal (mental) role—to focus on developing his mind. The personal role is you taking care of yourself!

As we mentioned earlier, many people have set professional goals at some point. However, thinking about your goals in the context of your different roles helps you balance success stories across each area of your life. When you divide your life into your most important roles, you can maintain balance and think about what you can do to achieve your vision in each role. This approach keeps you focused on your priorities and what matters most (Q2).

3. Set one to four SMART goals in each role.

You've likely heard of the SMART acronym at some point in your career; it's nothing new. However, what the acronym really means is new for most people.

Writing goals in a SMART way is key to effective goal setting and one of the most challenging areas to get right; it is definitely a skillset. As with anything, the more you practice writing goals this way, the easier it becomes. How you write your goals sets you up for either success or failure.

In an interesting study, Strava, a software company that tracks cycling and running exercises, tracked 98.3 million uploaded activities and found that the most common date for people to ditch their New Year's resolution is January 19th—just under three weeks into the year.[1] The study also observed that although most quit on January 19th, 88 percent of runners who set a specific goal were still running six months later. This is why we shared in the previous chapter that people are significantly more likely to accomplish something when they ditch the proverbial New Year's resolution and write their goals in a way that sets them up for success.

To that point, your words and how you write your goals matter! There is a big difference between *Get in better shape this year* and *Have a resting heart rate of 62 beats per minute by July 1st.*

Each team member should be able to identify the goals that matter most to them and write them correctly. Establishing roles and goals is a skillset that every manager and team member would benefit from mastering because it will directly impact their performance and productivity.

Let's go a little deeper into the SMART acronym and see how these examples might apply to you:

SPECIFIC

The more specific a goal is, the more likely you are to achieve it. Which of these common goals do you think is worded better?

- *Lose weight.*
- *Be at 135 pounds by October 30th.*

The second example is better, of course, because it is specific and easier to develop a plan around. Furthermore, the second example is written positively. Positive goals feel more achievable and are more motivating than negative ones. Notice how the example did not say *Lose 15 pounds*; instead, it stated a specific target weight. Weight is just one example that people often use; the same concept could apply to other areas of your health, relationships, and the like.

These little adjustments to the wording might seem obvious here. Still, it is common to see variations of the *lose weight* goal in the professional setting, and then people wonder why they don't see dramatic improvements. Wording matters!

MEASURABLE

At the end of the year, you should be able to look back at your goals and objectively say, "Yes, I did" or "No, I didn't" accomplish them. Two words you should never use when setting goals are *more* and *better*—or any variation of those vague words. A measurable goal increases accountability and is more likely to help you accomplish it.

Here are two examples to illustrate the difference between a measurable goal and one that isn't:

- *Have a great relationship with my spouse.*
- *Average two dates a month without the children.*

Or:

- *Read more books.*
- *Read 12 personal growth books by December 20th.*

The second example in both cases is a better goal because it is specific *and* measurable. The example of a great relationship is a nice vision, but it's not a goal because it is neither specific nor measurable. Likewise, the first example in both cases allows for wiggle room. However, the second examples promote accountability because they are either "yes" or "no" goals—they drive behavior and action.

ACHIEVABLE

Your goals should stretch you and potentially take you outside your comfort zone but still be achievable. It may not be realistic to set a goal to finish a marathon in the next three months if you've never run in your life. If a goal is unachievable or even just too difficult, you're more likely to become discouraged and give up. Remember the rubber band discussion in Chapter 1? Our goals should stretch us yet still be achievable. A phrase we like to use is that your goals should cause you to feel slightly uncomfortable. Slightly uncomfortable is a good balance between stretching us and still being achievable.

When the trainer asked the sales team from Chapter 1 to go from 17 to 34 sales, they were definitely a little uncomfortable knowing that would stretch them. That's the balance you're looking for—slightly uncomfortable, coupled with excitement and focus.

RELEVANT

Your goals should be relevant and aligned with your vision. If a part of your vision is *I am a healthy and well-rounded person*, then you would likely include specific goals about health and exercise. Your goals are the milestones toward achieving your vision.

TIME-SPECIFIC

If possible, add a date or time to your goal. For example, *Finish a 5k in less than 30 minutes by July 21st*, or *Average two dates a month.* Attaching a time or date to your goal increases accountability. We'll say this a couple more times, but the word *average* is a great word that gives you flexibility while still being time-specific. For example, *Read every day for 15 minutes* doesn't give you any flexibility or grace, whereas *Read an average of one growth book per month* does. Whether it's related to health, relationships, work, or anything else, the word *average* offers you some flexibility while still giving you a focal point. We'll come back to that again shortly.

4. Send your goals to three to five people you trust.

Once you develop your goals, consider sending them to three to five people you trust and respect. Sharing your goals is one of the keys to accountability. Several studies indicate this step significantly increases the likelihood of a person accomplishing their goals. You can tell them why you are sending them your goals and then report back to them at the end of the year—it's a simple ask and requires almost nothing on their part. We have shared our roles and goals for decades, which has helped us form a tight bond with that circle of friends. Your peers will enjoy getting your goals and your report from the previous year.

We can tell you from firsthand experience that when we are waffling on whether to finish a goal halfway through the year, remembering this year-end reporting usually drives us to complete the goal.

Pause and think of a few people with whom you could share your goals. Whoever you visualize, do you respect and admire them? If so, that's the type of accountability team you want.

This crucial step of sharing your goals will almost always increase your likelihood of accomplishing them.

5. Reference your goals often.

Lastly, don't make all the effort to develop your goals and then tuck them in a drawer somewhere. You've heard the saying, "Out of sight, out of mind." Instead, put your goals where you can see them often, such as in your paper or digital planner. Ultimately, it all comes down to pre-week planning, which you'll read about in the next two chapters. The most successful people—those who see dramatic improvements—reference their goals weekly as part of their pre-week planning. The whole point is to make our daily and weekly actions align with our goals and vision. People love the Do What Matters Most structure because the vision, goals, and pre-week planning work harmoniously together, and being able to reference them in a one-stop shop (their planner) boosts their odds of success.

The Slight Edge of Goal Setting

There is a great book written by Jeff Olson titled *The Slight Edge*. The whole point of the book is that a couple of small tweaks or variations in almost anything can have a massive impact on the outcome—hence, the slight edge. For example, a door swings on small hinges. There may be little movement near the hinge but significant movement at the outer portion of the door. Writing goals the right way is a similar concept. Making a few minor tweaks or variations to the old way of goal writing can have a significant impact on the outcome. In the spirit of setting goals in a powerful way that drives a specific behavior, we invite you to avoid the term *New Year's resolution* for the reasons mentioned earlier. As you'll see, a few slight adjustments will change a vague New Year's resolution into a focused goal. The differences are subtle yet significant, giving you an enormous edge.

Following the five goal-setting steps from this chapter will help you develop clarity, focus, and balance. Remember, words matter, and the words you use in your goals will often mean the difference between success and failure; the seemingly small adjustments are the slight edge. The subconscious mind is powerful, and if you're "failing" on enough of your written goals, your subconscious mind will nudge you not to look at them anymore because doing so brings out associated feelings of guilt. When you pick your words carefully, however, your subconscious mind can work *for* you instead of against you.

In addition to the five steps, here are a few other guidelines and tips to set you up for success in your goal setting.

Rarely set daily goals.

When we share this tip, a handful of people always skeptically raise their eyebrows . . . until we elaborate. In roles and goals, the focus is on your *annual* goals. The tactical focus comes during pre-week planning—discussed in Chapters 8 and 9—and will help you prioritize what matters most at the daily/weekly level, eliminating the need for an annual goal that uses the word *daily*. For example, some people start the year excitedly proclaiming their resolution to *Exercise for 30 minutes every day*. They don't realize that they've likely just set themselves up for failure. If they miss a single day, they have already "failed" in their goal, as worded. As we just noted, with enough "failures," most people subconsciously quit looking at their goals and go back to whatever they were doing before. This type of wording is one of the reasons so many New Year's resolutions get tossed out two to three weeks into the year.

By making a couple of small adjustments to their goals, they can set themselves up for success. For example, they might word their goal this way: *Average four 30-minute workouts per week* or *Run a 10k by September 1st*. If we are talking about making a sales goal, they might shift their goal from *Make 30 sales calls every day* to *Average 150 sales calls weekly* or *Achieve $1.2M in sales by December 26th*. Notice how the slight wording adjustments provide more flexibility in time and actions? The adjusted examples add flexibility during the week while still maintaining the material integrity of what the goal is trying to accomplish.

This is not to say that you cannot or should not break down a monthly or quarterly goal into daily targets. For example, if we want to make 20 monthly sales, we would likely break that down into daily and weekly numbers to achieve the monthly goal. However, for this approach, let's focus on your annual goals.

With this tip, we're simply saying that because of pre-week planning, there are very few cases when you should have a *daily* goal—a goal that fails if you miss a single day—as part of your annual goals.

Give yourself flexibility.

Think again about the previous example. Someone with the daily sales goal of *Make 30 sales calls every day* only has to make fewer than 30 calls on one single day, for whatever reason, to fail at their goal. If they make a small adjustment in wording, however, they can maintain the same standard but have more flexibility. One way to do this is to use the word *average*, which, as we noted earlier in this chapter, can be powerful in goal setting. In most cases, the goal *Average 30 sales calls per day* maintains the material integrity of the goal yet gives the person a little flexibility to be off on one or two days without "failing." As another example, in the role of spouse or partner, dating goals are common—and rightfully so. Shifting slightly from *Go on at least 3 dates a month* to *Average 3 dates a month* provides huge subconscious flexibility in a seemingly small change.

Another way to give yourself some more flexibility is to be careful with the words *every* and *at least*. There's a place for those words; you just need to be cautious using them. Instead of saying *every day* or *do x at least x number of times*, you can stretch the time horizon on your goal. For example, from the last chapter, Gary was going to initially write the goal *Read at least 15 minutes per day.* You can see there was no flexibility in Gary's original goal, and it would take only missing one day for him to fail.

Instead, with a small tweak, Gary changed the goal to *Average reading 1 personal growth book per month*—which is what he did. He could have also written the goal as *Read 12 personal growth books by December 26th*, achieving the same objective. You might think it's still important to read each day, and you're right. Gary used pre-week planning to allocate a few minutes to read most days, but as expected, he missed a few days. Writing the goal as

Average reading 1 personal growth book per month still maintained the intent of the goal, and it set Gary up for success by giving him flexibility. Remember, pre-week planning will connect your goals to the daily and weekly levels.

Set one to four goals in each role.

The intent is to focus on what matters most. If *everything* matters, then nothing matters. Keeping it to one to four goals per role will help you decide what matters most in each role. If this is your first time writing your goals, maybe you can start with one goal per role. If you're comfortable with goal setting, maybe you can come up with three or four goals per role. Remember, goals that stretch you should feel slightly uncomfortable.

In most cases, setting more than four goals per role detracts from the whole point of this process: to help you focus your time and energy on what matters most. For best results, get laser-focused on the one or two goals that matter most to you in each role.

At the end of the process, you should feel excitement, focus, and, if you've stretched yourself, slight discomfort.

If you haven't taken the free Do What Matters Most productivity assessment discussed in the introduction, consider doing it now. It only takes a few minutes and will give you a great snapshot of where you are today in your personal role (physically, mentally, emotionally, and spiritually). You can access the assessment at BYBAssessment.com. It will assist you in pinpointing areas of focus so you can identify the most meaningful goals for each role.

Aim for 70 to 80 percent accomplishment.

Traditionally, goal setting is often viewed as an all-or-nothing approach. However, giving yourself grace and flexibility while still stretching is important. After years of studying goal setting, we've found that a 70 to 80 percent accomplishment target seems to strike the right balance between stretching yourself and aiming too high. If you easily accomplish all your goals, you could have stretched yourself further. If you accomplish only 20 to 30 percent of your goals, you likely had too many goals, didn't word them correctly, or didn't do pre-week planning. A 70 to 80 percent accomplishment rate at year-end usually correlates to a dramatic jump in productivity, well-being, and a sense of accomplishment. If you don't accomplish 100 percent of your goals, that's alright. It doesn't mean you didn't give 100 percent effort; it simply reflects the reality that life happens. Allowing for flexibility is part of the process.

Plan for one to two hours to finish your roles and goals.

It usually takes people between one and two hours to finish their roles and goals. We invite you to block time in your calendar right now to go through this process. Procrastination is one of the most insidious success killers, and many people have never made it past the phase of good intentions. Therefore, the best time to start is right now, while it is fresh in your mind.

Og Mandino, author of *The Greatest Salesman in the World*, wisely said, "I will not avoid the tasks of today, for I know that tomorrow never comes. Let me act now even though my actions may not bring happiness or success, for it is better to act and fail than not to act and flounder."[2]

In business, *return on investment (ROI)* is one of the most important indicators to track. Developing your roles and goals is an investment in yourself and will yield a tremendous ROI. One to two hours is a small investment of time for an improved, balanced, and successful life. Wouldn't you agree?

Do this with your partner or team.

If your partner, family, or team is willing to participate, you can begin to imagine how much more powerful the outcome will be when everyone is aligned using a similar process. When you have a team composed of members who have each developed their roles and goals and consistently do pre-week planning, it creates unity, alignment, and accountability. For example, organizations that participate in the Do What Matters Most training are usually invited to hold a meeting at the beginning of each week to align their team on what matters most (Q2) that week. Imagine if each team member developed their roles and goals and did pre-week planning before that weekly alignment meeting—that would make for an aligned team and one we'd want to be a part of!

Get the right tools.

If you want to drive a nail into a pole, it certainly helps to have a hammer. Likewise, when developing your vision and goals and doing pre-week planning, it helps to use the right tools. If you invested in a planner using the links in the introduction, you've already seen how valuable it is to have a central place to reference your vision and goals and do pre-week planning. Anything you can do to promote consistency and make them more easily accessible often increases your focus and the likelihood of maintaining these habits throughout the rest of your life. If you haven't invested in one and would like to, visit DoWhatMattersMostPlanner.com. We'll reiterate that you don't have to purchase these tools; you can do this work on a blank piece of paper. However, those who go on to make these lifelong habits usually invest in the tools.

If you have a paper or digital planner, we encourage you to put your finalized vision and goals there. This way, your planner is your go-to, one-stop shop for your organization and what matters most. Figure 16 on page 108 shows what a completed Vision and Goals page might look like in your paper planner.

Practice

Let's say someone you know wants to learn how to play basketball but has never touched an actual basketball. If you spend all day talking about basketball with them, but they still don't touch the ball, they'll likely never learn how to play. Wouldn't you agree that they need to practice dribbling, shooting, and so on to learn? Like anything, if we want to develop a new skillset, it takes practice.

In the spirit of practice and repetition, let's review a few examples focused on creating SMART goals and using some slight-edge tips. Imagine you're a leader or coworker mentoring a team member to improve their goals. Or, maybe you're a parent helping your son or daughter with their goals. How would you rephrase each of these examples to make them well-written goals?

1. Be a better friend.
2. Exercise every day to improve my well-being.

3. Be a better leader.
4. Improve sales and do a better job closing deals.
5. Be healthier this year and lose more weight.
6. Get better feedback from my team.
7. Be more mindful and focus on meditating every day.
8. Spend more quality time with my spouse or partner.

Now, consider how you would reword each goal based on what we've covered in this chapter. For example, notice how the words *more* and *better* keep showing up; those two words should never be used in goals because they are neither specific nor measurable. You probably also noticed the words *every day*. If you were mentoring someone, what would you change to improve the wording of these goals?

The following list shows variations for each goal from the previous list. Notice how these are both specific and measurable while also allowing flexibility:

1. Average two lunches a month with a friend.
2. Average three strength workouts per week.
3. Finish the annual strategic plan for the marketing division by January 27th.
4. Achieve $642,000 in sales by December 26th. Another way to write this might be *Average 46 sales calls per week*.
5. Run a 5k before July 30th.
6. Do a continue–start–stop with my team before March 1st.
7. Average three meditations per week.
8. Average two dates a month without the children.

Can you see in these few examples how much words matter? How you write your goals sets you up for either success or failure. Armed with this new skillset, you're ready to start the process of developing your roles and goals.

Figure 16. A completed Vision and Goals page

PRODUCTIVITY • TIME-MANAGEMENT • LEADERSHIP

EXAMPLE VISION & GOALS

MY PERSONAL VISION AND GOALS

"You will either lead a life by design or live a life by default!"

Role: Personal (Physical, Mental, Emotional, Spiritual)

Vision: I live a balanced, healthy lifestyle, and I am in great physical shape. I nurture my soul and live with purpose. I am financially free with no debt or financial obligations to anyone.

GOAL(S):

Physical: Run a 10k by September 1st.
Average 72 BPM by July 1st.

Mental: Read at least 12 leadership or motivational books before December 30th.

Emotional: Average two yoga sessions per week.

Spiritual: Average one nature walk per week.

Role: Manager

Vision: I am a great manager who contributes to an outstanding team. I am a key player who always brings energy, enthusiasm, and a no-quit attitude to the team. I uplift the people that I work with and help them to become their best.

Goal(s): 1. Finalize the strategic plan for our division by February 1st.
2. Do a Continue - Start - Stop with all employees by April 1st.
3. Achieve $1.5M in sales by December 27th.

PRODUCTIVITY • TIME-MANAGEMENT • LEADERSHIP

EXAMPLE VISION & GOALS

Role: Parent

Vision: I am an example in thought and deed of a kind and caring person. I am the type of person I want my children to grow up to be. I am present with my children and continuously develop memories together. I invest time and energy to help them see their potential, bring out their best, and how they can make a difference in the world.

Goal(s): 1. Average one family weekend trip within five hours of our home every other month.
2. Take each kid on at least one one-on-one trip before December 30th.
3. Help each child finish their Roles and Goals by January 10th.

Role: Spouse or Partner

Vision: I am a kind and caring spouse who always helps my husband/wife/partner feel like a 10! I am totally faithful in thought and action and constantly strive to compliment, serve, and be the husband/wife/partner of his/her dreams.

Goal(s): 1. Read Start with the Vision together and go through the Six-Step Process by July 1st.
2. At least two weekend getaway trips together before December 30th.
3. Average two dates a month without the children.

Role:

Vision:

Goal(s):

Wrap Up

There's an association of ironworkers and contractors with more than 500,000 members. They've trained hundreds of their members in the Do What Matters Most program. It's a fantastic group of people; they're dedicated, loyal, and hardworking. At the same time, the demands of their profession have taken a heavy toll on many of them, with events like divorce, suicide, and personal challenges being way more common than any of them would like. It's been interesting to see their feedback; many wished they could have learned this skillset in their 20s because of how life-changing it's been for them. A lot of them noted that it would have dramatically improved their relationships, work–life balance, well-being, and purpose for living. One ironworker, who went through the course twice, said, "The first time through, I wasn't in the right mindset to apply the habits. The second time through, I'm in a totally different place, and this has been life-changing."

What's changed in the lives of so many ironworkers and contractors? Rather than just going through the daily grind and getting burned out, they've stepped back to identify what matters most to them—their vision and goals in each respective role. They've started prioritizing their own well-being, relationships, and other areas of their lives as much as they have their professional lives.

Some might think this would detract from their job, but it's the exact opposite. When their personal lives are in a healthy place, many have shared that it frees them up emotionally so they can be present at work and have more energy throughout the day. If you think about it, a person's attitude is substantially different when they have balance in their various roles versus just grinding through each day. As we shared in an earlier chapter, our research has showed that people are 40 percent more productive in the workplace when they are balanced in their various roles.

So, whether it's an ironworker, someone in your organization, a family member, or, most importantly, you, it's time to start on your roles and goals.

If you read this in November or December, we suggest you develop your goals for the coming year. If you read this in any other month, we encourage you to develop your roles and goals for the remainder of this year.

Look at your roles and goals through the lens of the ping-pong balls and the aquarium example from Chapter 3. There was plenty of room when the teacher put the ping-pong balls in the aquarium before the pebbles, sand, or water. When the teacher put the water in the aquarium first, there was no room for ping-pong balls. Like the teacher in this experiment, you want to prevent the small things from crowding out the big things. The idea is to proactively identify the things that matter most—your roles and goals—so they don't get crowded out by the daily fires or the next shiny object.

Let's finish this chapter with some variations of the questions from earlier in this section:

- What goals could you develop this year to expand your circle of peace and balance?
- How will you specifically measure success this year in the different roles of your life?
- What are some ways you could increase your contribution in your workplace? How can you measure those?
- When will you finish your roles and goals?
- Where will you put your roles and goals so you see them often?
- If you choose to share your goals, who will you share them with?

These are the questions to get you started. The art truly is in the start. You don't have to be perfect at this; just getting some initial thoughts on paper can often be life-changing. Many people have told us that just thinking about them was a great start, and that's true. However, writing them in your planner (physical or digital) and referencing them often is a big step up from just thinking about them. It also significantly increases the likelihood of you doing and accomplishing them. Consider blocking off a time in your calendar to finalize your roles and goals while it's fresh in your mind.

Now it's time to move on to pre-week planning—what we consider to be the most important habit because it brings everything together. Your vision and goals have been the process of *identifying* what matters most; pre-week planning is the *doing*. It's what empowers you to accomplish your vision and goals.

REFLECTION QUESTIONS FOR THIS CHAPTER

1. What was the experience of developing your roles and goals like for you?
2. What are your most important roles?
3. Do your roles and goals positively impact each area of your circle of peace and balance?
4. Who else do you know that would benefit from going through this process to develop their roles and goals (child, partner, team member)? Why would this process be helpful to them?

8

The Power of Pre-week Planning

Before a pilot jumps into the cockpit, they always do their pre-flight planning. In the fighter pilot world, it takes one to ten hours to plan a single mission, depending on its complexity. Pre-flight planning includes researching the target or destination, planning the route of flight, checking the weather, and more.

Imagine what would happen if a pilot said, "We don't need to do pre-flight planning; we're just going to wing it!" That would result in chaos, frustration, misalignment, and confusion—not good!

How often do people go into their week without a plan and expect a different result? Just as *pre-flight* planning is critical for a pilot, *pre-week* planning is essential for anyone who wants to take control of their life and do what matters most. If a pilot wants to be successful, they do their pre-flight planning. How much more successful and balanced would you be if you approached your professional and personal life like a pilot—doing your pre-week planning before you start the week? When it comes to productivity, pre-week planning is the *keystone* (the most important stone in an arch); it's what drives the vision and goals to become a reality. Pre-week planning is the key to scheduling your priorities rather than prioritizing your schedule.

If you met us on the street one day and asked, "What's one habit that would change my life—guaranteed?" our answer would almost always be pre-week planning. When people consistently do pre-week planning, productivity increases, health and relationships improve, and stress and task saturation decrease.

To that point, our research shows that a person who does pre-week planning will accomplish 20 more priorities in a week, which translates into accomplishing 800 to 1,000 more priorities in a year, than they would have without pre-week planning—all with less stress! As we mentioned in Chapter 1, it's easy to get lost in the numbers until you remember that those priorities include exercise, doctor's appointments, date nights, family time, important client calls, time spent with team members, and so many more. In other words, they're not just numbers; these things will ultimately become your dash! We'll cover this research in more detail later in this chapter.

In the spirit of *good, better, best*, we invite you to see how pre-week planning can enhance and improve whatever planning approach you're using today. If you've been using sticky notes or a running to-do list, pre-week planning will take it to the next level. No matter your position or title, everyone in an organization will benefit from the simplicity of pre-week planning.

Years ago, a Do What Matters Most certified trainer led the training with the executive team of PepsiCo. Each executive developed a draft of their personal vision, as well as their roles and goals. The energy and excitement in the room were palpable!

The trainer moved into pre-week planning and taught them the four steps to it. Each person then took about 10 minutes to do their pre-week planning for the upcoming week. One of the executives, whom we'll call John, wrote in the role of parent, "Call my son." John was in his late 50s to early 60s and was a seasoned executive who had been with the company for decades.

It was not abnormal to see someone write "Call my son" or its equivalent in that role; nonetheless, the trainer asked John why he specifically wrote that. He responded, "Because I haven't talked with my son in seven years!" It was apparent this issue had weighed on him for a long time. He continued, "My son and I got into an argument seven years ago, and we haven't spoken since." Wow!

The trainer asked John when he would make the call that week, and he responded, "I'll call him Wednesday evening." The trainer then invited John to write it in his weekly planner for Wednesday at 7:00 p.m., which he did.

Six months later, at a follow-up workshop with this same executive team, John jumped out of his chair to greet the trainer. They shook hands, and the trainer asked him, "So, did you make the call?" John responded enthusiastically, "I was scared to pick up the phone that evening. I had no idea whether or not my son would even talk with me." He continued, "But I made the call. It was amazing because as soon as we started talking, we realized neither of us could remember what we had argued about seven years ago. Now, we talk every week, and we've become best friends!" He shared that he discovered on that call he had two grandchildren he didn't even know existed.

It was interesting to hear some of John's additional thoughts. He commented, "For years, I knew I needed to make that call, but like many things, I woke up every morning thinking I would just do it the next day. Weeks turned into months, and months turned into years. I intended to make the call but always seemed too busy, so I kept putting it off until later." He also said, "Since I've repaired that relationship, my entire world has changed. I'm more focused at work. I'm a better leader and have a renewed energy I didn't have before! It's as if an invisible weight lifted from my shoulders." He concluded by saying, "Without pre-week planning, I probably wouldn't have made that call. I never thought about planning my weeks through the lens of my different roles, especially the role of father. Pre-week planning seems so simple, yet it changed my life in almost every way!"

There are many Johns in the world, even though the specific situations might differ. How often do we put off or procrastinate doing what matters most? Another way to think about that is to ask what the impact is of not doing those important things.

Remember, in our research of thousands of people, 68 percent felt prioritizing their time was their number one challenge, yet 80 percent didn't feel their current approach to time management was working well. That's a big gap. Identifying your vision, developing your roles and goals, and *especially* doing pre-week planning are the answer to closing that gap. They give you a structured approach and the right tools to schedule your priorities and lead a life by design.

The Pre-week Planning Research

Earlier in the book, we said that people who finish their vision and goals and are disciplined about pre-week planning would see an average increase in productivity of 30 to 50 percent. That is only partly true. The real improvement is actually much higher than that!

Figure 17 shows the results of our study of people who did pre-week planning for five weeks. It is important to note that these results came *after* the participants developed their vision and goals. In other words, pre-week planning was done in alignment with the vision and goals rather than as an isolated event. It's also worth pointing out that most people in this study did some form of weekly planning (sticky notes, to-do lists, ABC priorities, etc.) before learning about this program. However, most participants didn't feel like their approach was very effective. In many cases, their planning focused *only* on their professional role. So, planning their weeks around their respective roles was new for most of them, as it is for 96 percent of people participating in the Do What Matters Most training.

Figure 17. The results of pre-week planning for one month

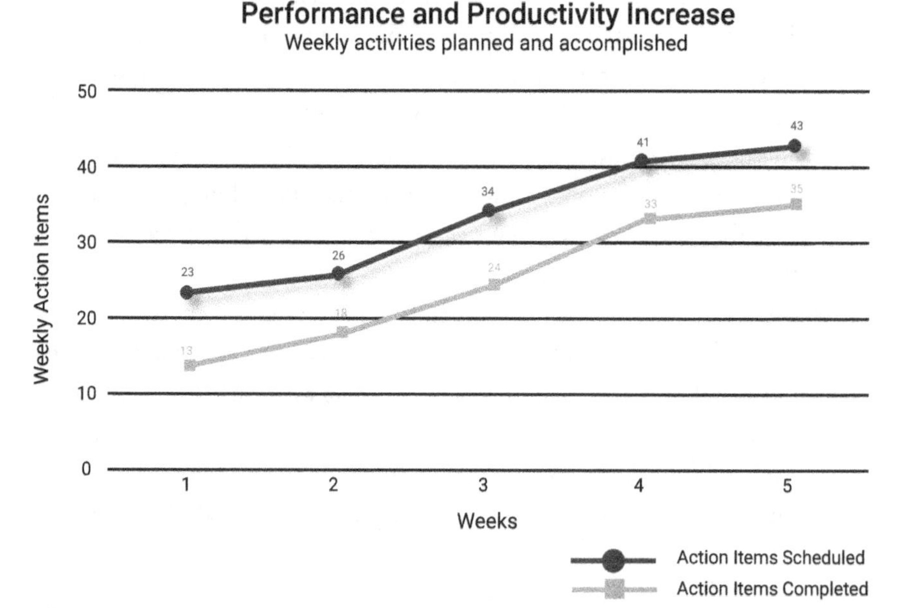

The vertical axis in Figure 17 tracks weekly action items, and the horizontal axis refers to the number of weeks tracked. The rising line on the top represents weekly action items *scheduled* as part of pre-week planning, and the rising line on the bottom represents the weekly action items *accomplished* at the end of the week.

Here are four key takeaways from our pre-week planning research:

1. Like anything, pre-week planning is a skillset. The more we do it, the better we become at it. With each repetition, it becomes easier and takes less effort.

   Let's use a sports analogy to illustrate this point. If someone learns a new technique, such as catching a football, they won't get it perfectly right on the first try. Doing it correctly takes numerous repetitions until it becomes a part of their habits. The more they practice correctly, the easier it becomes. The same is true of pre-week planning.

   Take a look at Figure 17. You see an average of 23 weekly action items scheduled for the first week (the 23 planned action items include the action items added up from all their roles); this number swells to 41 weekly action items planned by the fourth week. Again, as in the football example, this increase results from practice and repetition. When people do pre-week planning for one or two weeks, their brains naturally get used to it, and the ideas flow a lot easier. With time, they think of more ideas and become more creative in each role, which increases their performance and productivity. The more familiar you become with something, the easier and more natural it is. You start to figure out your techniques or variations and get into a rhythm. This familiarity with pre-week planning is why teams see a significant increase in engagement, performance, and productivity, even in the first 30 days after implementing these new habits.

   Because developing a new habit is a function of consistency and repetition, it takes time. We'll mention this more than once, but it's crucial to give yourself grace. In other words, if you miss a week or even several weeks, that's all right. You'll certainly notice the difference between the weeks you do pre-week planning and those you don't.

So, if you miss a week or two, you can pick up where you left off. Later in the book, we'll share additional tips on sustaining momentum and consistency. The bottom line is that once pre-week planning becomes a habit, you'll never want to live without it!

2. The number of weekly action items *accomplished* will also dramatically increase in the first month of pre-week planning. As previously mentioned, the first few weeks are for developing the habit and figuring out what works best for you—for example, finding a consistent time to do pre-week planning or deciding whether you like the paper planner or digital planner better. In this timeframe, you're dipping a toe into the water to see what works best for you. After that, you're usually used to the process and have determined the right approach for you.

   As you look at Figure 17, notice that in the first week, only an average of 13 weekly action items were accomplished, and by the fourth week, that number more than doubled to 33. This shows that when pre-week planning is done consistently and correctly for just one month, it can lead to more than a 100 percent increase in productivity, or in other words, priorities accomplished.

   Eventually, the number of action items planned and accomplished will level out. A typical person doing pre-week planning plans an average of 40 to 45 action items into their week, which is the sum of all their action items across their respective roles. That's up from just 23 action items planned and 13 accomplished in their first week doing pre-week planning.

3. Another observation from the research is that well-being, work–life balance, and happiness are significantly higher when people do pre-week planning. Typically, that's because they're planning their weeks through the lens of their most important roles rather than just their professional role. The number one comment people make after doing pre-week planning for the first time is something along the lines of, "I've done pre-week planning in my professional role, but I've

never thought about planning my week through the lens of my other roles." The overall increase in productivity makes sense when you think about it. When someone makes time to exercise, read, meditate, and so on, other areas of their life will also improve. You've probably experienced or seen this when taking care of yourself first; it gives you the energy and bandwidth to be effective in your other roles. It is much easier to show up for your team, coworkers, and clients when your own house is in order. The term we used earlier in the book for this was *performance average* or the *compounding effect*. Doing pre-week planning by role will increase your performance average—and because of this compounding effect, almost every area of your circle of peace and balance will improve.

The focus on overall well-being may seem obvious, but things like exercise, reading, relationship building, and meditation often slip through the cracks for many people. However, when they shift to Q2 thinking and planning, they make time for what matters most, and their overall productivity increases.

4. A final observation from the research shown in Figure 17 is that in just one month, the gap between weekly action items planned and accomplished narrows significantly. Notice in the first week of pre-week planning, only 56 percent of the planned weekly action items were completed; however, by the fourth week, 80 percent were accomplished. We call that number the *productivity quotient*—the result of dividing the number of action items planned by those accomplished.

   The target productivity quotient is between 70 and 80 percent, the same as it is for our roles and goals. Q1 fires will always pop up during the week, and life happens, so this target accounts for both eventualities. The expectation we set is to rarely plan to accomplish 100 percent of your planned weekly action items, not because of a lack of effort, but to give yourself grace and account for life happening. If you're the type of person who likes to check every square and cross off every item, it's especially important to give yourself permission to be flexible and adjust during the week.

Although it's always nice to see the research and statistical side of these three powerful habits, the real benefit comes when you see the transformation happening to those on your team and in your family, and especially when you see it happening in your own life. Every one of those "numbers" you see in the weekly action items represents a meaningful activity or task you have accomplished. Every number represents something you've done to improve the team, your health, your relationship, or another important part of your life.

Allow us to share our friend Rich's story. He worked for Schluter Systems, a leader in installation systems for tile and stone. Shortly after he finished the Do What Matters Most course, Rich sent us a handwritten note. His comments are summarized here to illustrate what happens when a person applies the habits of vision, roles and goals, and pre-week planning together:

> My name is Rich, and I met you about a year ago at our Schluter meeting in Florida. You trained over 100 of us. One of the first things you said at our event was that this day would "change my life!" At 64, this old dog can be rather skeptical. I am also one of Schluter's workshop presenters and felt that making such a claim to a large group was tough to pull off. But our leaders were willing to invest in me, so I decided to get their money's worth!
>
> You talked about the five most important things to a long and healthy life, and I was only doing three of those things. The two I wasn't focused on were meditation and sleep. As a result of vision, goals, and pre-week planning, I enrolled in a meditation training course and have been practicing it twice a day.
>
> Also, getting eight hours of sleep has always been impossible for me, and it seems harder the older I get. I set a goal to get a sleep test and investigate my options. It was determined that I have sleep apnea, so I recently got a CPAP device. Yes, it HAS been a game-changer! I'm sleeping better than ever and have a lot more energy throughout the day.
>
> The vision, goals, and pre-week planning helped me focus on what matters most and make important changes in my life! Thank you.

Rich had these ideas and intentions floating around in his mind for years, but the combination of the vision, goals, and pre-week planning (and his willing mindset) moved him to take action.

Another friend, Nicole, is a commercial designer with several young children at home. She and her husband, Jay, attended a Do What Matters Most workshop. Both commented that their marriage had suffered because of all the demands of life. Nicole's personal life was also affecting her professional life. She was not responding to people's business inquiries like she wanted, and her business suffered. She lost clients, felt task-saturated, and was constantly in Q1 and Q3. She was trying to balance raising her children, having a positive relationship with her husband, building her business, and finding time for herself. Needless to say, this was a challenging phase of life for Nicole.

After completing the course, Nicole and Jay decided to finalize their vision and goals and commit to pre-week planning to see its impact. They heard the promises, stories, and research but wanted to see if it would work for them.

Nicole later shared that when she does pre-week planning, she is on top of her game, her productivity is high, and she experiences minimal stress. Client relationships and referrals have improved, and she has seen significant growth in her business. During the handful of weeks when Nicole didn't do pre-week planning, she was stressed, anxious, and unproductive. Both she and Jay credit these habits, especially pre-week planning, with helping them take control of their chaotic schedules and prioritize what matters most. They also credit vision, goals, and pre-week planning with transforming their marriage and bringing the flame back into their relationship. They were living in Q1 and Q3, and when they learned about this program, they shifted to Q2 and purposefully focused on their priorities (what mattered most).

Another example of the powerful impact of pre-week planning is from Michelle, a certified trainer and an executive in a global organization based in the UK. She said the following:

> It's hard to believe I started doing this only a year ago. A major change in my life is pre-week planning. I have always done planning and had a "to-do" list, but it was never tied to my vision and goals (especially by role). I created a personal vision and goals that supported each of my roles. I have been doing that for a year and just finished using my first weekly planner. I can honestly say that I am more focused now and accomplishing things that were always important but that I put off or never got around

> to doing. I have focused time each week on the things that are important to me and are moving me toward accomplishing my goals and supporting my personal vision.
>
> Things seem to have started coming into being since I created my vision and have been doing pre-week planning. I smile to myself now every time something happens to move me toward my goals without a clear explanation.
>
> I've ordered books and planners for my team and family. I even gave one to my son, who is in his early 20s, and I see him now doing pre-week planning with a very well-defined vision and goals for himself. Amazing things are happening for him as well because of this focus. If you are a parent of a college grad, you know how exciting this is!

We could fill a book with messages from people who have shared the impact of these habits on their lives. Our hope in sharing these experiences with you is to foster a belief and confidence that you can do it. Anyone with the right mindset (a desire and discipline) can learn this skillset, which will be transformational.

Before we jump into *how* to do pre-week planning, it's essential to remember that it's all three of these habits together that create a chemistry of excellence. Pre-week planning is undoubtedly a game-changer, yet it is exponentially more powerful when aligned with the vision and goals. We hope you have already put some serious thought into your vision and goals by this point. When you finish them, pre-week planning aligns your daily and weekly activities with accomplishing your goals. Pre-week planning is the galvanizer of the three habits.

How to Be Successful with Pre-week Planning

Having seen thousands of people develop the habit of pre-week planning, we've learned some tips and ideas along the way that might also be helpful to you. We'll briefly share those before we get into the *how-to* of pre-week planning:

- **Give yourself grace.** We've mentioned this multiple times throughout the book, and there's a reason we keep repeating it. It's important to understand that pre-week planning is a process and a habit. Like any habit, it takes time to develop. You might miss a week here or there, but that doesn't mean you're giving up and quitting. It just means you're human, and it's an opportunity to get back on the proverbial horse. You'll find the more consistent you are, the better your weeks and overall life will be. When you miss a week, you'll clearly notice the difference. But, again, we're humans, and perfection isn't the expectation. Instead, this is the beginning of a journey, and everyone develops this habit at a different pace. The sooner you do, the sooner you'll notice a feeling of peace, control, and focus week in and week out—even with a productivity quotient of 70 to 80 percent!

- **Invest in a digital or physical planner.** It doesn't matter whether you use a paper planner or a digital planner; it's the *process* that's important. The pre-week planning process stays the same, *regardless* of whether you use the online or paper approach. The tools are part of what makes Do What Matters Most so unique. The ability to do pre-week planning within your existing Outlook or Chrome calendar is a game changer in developing the habit. Likewise, if you prefer paper, it's significantly easier to do pre-week planning when your planner is set up for you to plan your weeks around your roles. If you want to go your own route, you'll need to find a way to set up a system so you can easily reference your vision and goals each week and do pre-week planning around your roles.

  If you want to install the online planner with your Outlook or Chrome calendar or customize and design your own planner, visit DoWhatMattersMostPlanner.com.

- **Choose a time and set a reminder.** Whether you customize your own paper planner or use Outlook or Chrome, we suggest you choose a time that works best for you and then be consistent with that time. The process typically takes between 20 and 45 minutes, and most people set aside a block of time between Friday afternoon and Sunday evening (assuming a standard work schedule) to do it. If they wait until Monday morning, most people find it too late—the week's firestorm has already started, and Q1 is staring them in the face. Having said that, if you don't do your pre-week planning during the weekend, it's better to do it on Tuesday or Wednesday for the remainder of the week than not at all.

We invite you to think of the best time for you and set an alarm or reminder on your phone. In that reminder, type the words "pre-week planning." The alarm will serve as a reminder to connect the intention with developing the new habit. Those who set the alarm or reminder are much more likely to be consistent and develop the habit of pre-week planning. The key is to find a few minutes when you have some quiet time to yourself, such as a Saturday or Sunday morning.

- **Do pre-week planning as a team before the weekly alignment meeting.** The last tip for now is to hold a weekly alignment meeting with your team to start the week by ensuring that everyone is going in the same direction. It's like pre-week planning at an individual level but for the team. The teams that hold a weekly alignment meeting, and have everyone do their own pre-week planning *before* it, are aligned and in sync with each other. You can certainly expect team members to do pre-week planning before the meeting if they've all been trained in Do What Matters Most!

  Imagine your own team and how much better the working environment would be if you were ahead of the curve in Q2. Unnecessary fires wouldn't be popping up because the team will have addressed issues before they become fires. Remember, the team is the sum of each individual. So, if each individual—including the leader—is focused on what matters most, the entire team experiences a cultural transformation. They'll spend between 60 and 70 percent of their time in Q2 and a much smaller percentage in Q1, Q3, or Q4. As a result, they'll see significantly higher performance, productivity, and alignment.

These are just a few quick tips to set you and your team up for success with the habit of pre-week planning. In the next chapter, after we've explained how to do it, we'll share a few additional ideas on sustaining the momentum.

Wrap Up

Zig Ziglar once said, "I believe that being successful means having a balance of success stories across the many areas of your life. You can't truly be considered successful in your professional life if your home life is in shambles." We believe the essence of Zig's words is that a person's performance average will skyrocket when their various roles are in balance. And this balance isn't a myth—it's a reality that you can achieve through the right process and tools. Pre-week planning, as detailed in the next chapter, is that process. It's a habit that can transform your life, just like it did for John, the PepsiCo executive, when he resolved a relationship issue with his son and saw every area of his life improve.

Pre-week planning is not just a process; it's a beacon of hope for those struggling to manage their hectic schedules and prioritize what truly matters. It's a simple yet powerful approach that empowers you to take ownership of your life and lead a life by design. Imagine the possibilities, the freedom, and the peace of mind that come with such a structured approach.

In the next chapter, we'll introduce *how* to do pre-week planning!

REFLECTION QUESTIONS FOR THIS CHAPTER

1. How could pre-week planning positively impact your life?
2. What were your thoughts on time and pre-week planning while reading this chapter?
3. What would be the impact of helping your team members, friends, or family prioritize their time?

9

How to Do Pre-week Planning

You've heard us discuss pre-week planning throughout the book; now it's time to learn how to actually do it!

If you invested in a paper planner, please open it to the weekly view and follow along while reading this chapter. While we review each step, you can also reference the blank weekly planner template in Figure 18 or the completed template in Figure 19 (the arrows are for illustrative purposes only, demonstrating that you assign a time for each action item).

Figure 18. Blank pre-week planning template

MONTH: ______________

WEEK OF: ______________

Pre-Week Planning

1. Review your vision, annual goals, and calendar.
2. Write your roles (Personal, Work, Family, etc.).
3. Set action items for each role.
4. Schedule a time for each action item.

PRINCIPLE OF THE WEEK:

"If there is one secret of success, it is concentration. Effective executives do first things first, and they do one thing at a time."
— Peter F. Drucker

PRODUCTIVITY QUOTIENT:

Roles:	Personal						
ACTION ITEMS							

NOTES & LISTS

MONDAY

6:00 6:30 7:00 7:30 8:00 8:30 9:00 9:30 10:00 10:30 11:00 11:30 NOON 12:30 1:00 1:30 2:00 2:30 3:00 3:30 4:00 4:30 5:00 5:30 6:00 6:30 7:00 7:30 8:00 8:30 9:00 9:30

TUESDAY

6:00 6:30 7:00 7:30 8:00 8:30 9:00 9:30 10:00 10:30 11:00 11:30 NOON 12:30 1:00 1:30 2:00 2:30 3:00 3:30 4:00 4:30 5:00 5:30 6:00 6:30 7:00 7:30 8:00 8:30 9:00 9:30

WEDNESDAY

6:00 6:30 7:00 7:30 8:00 8:30 9:00 9:30 10:00 10:30 11:00 11:30 NOON 12:30 1:00 1:30 2:00 2:30 3:00 3:30 4:00 4:30 5:00 5:30 6:00 6:30 7:00 7:30 8:00 8:30 9:00 9:30

THURSDAY

6:00 6:30 7:00 7:30 8:00 8:30 9:00 9:30 10:00 10:30 11:00 11:30 NOON 12:30 1:00 1:30 2:00 2:30 3:00 3:30 4:00 4:30 5:00 5:30 6:00 6:30 7:00 7:30 8:00 8:30 9:00 9:30

FRIDAY

6:00 6:30 7:00 7:30 8:00 8:30 9:00 9:30 10:00 10:30 11:00 11:30 NOON 12:30 1:00 1:30 2:00 2:30 3:00 3:30 4:00 4:30 5:00 5:30 6:00 6:30 7:00 7:30 8:00 8:30 9:00 9:30

SATURDAY

SUNDAY

NOTES & LISTS

WEEKLY REVIEW

- What were my three biggest wins this week?
- What am I most proud of?
- How would I rate my week on a scale of 1-10? What can I improve on?
- What are three things I'm grateful for this week?
- What annual goal did I come closer to achieving this week?

Figure 19. A completed pre-week planning example

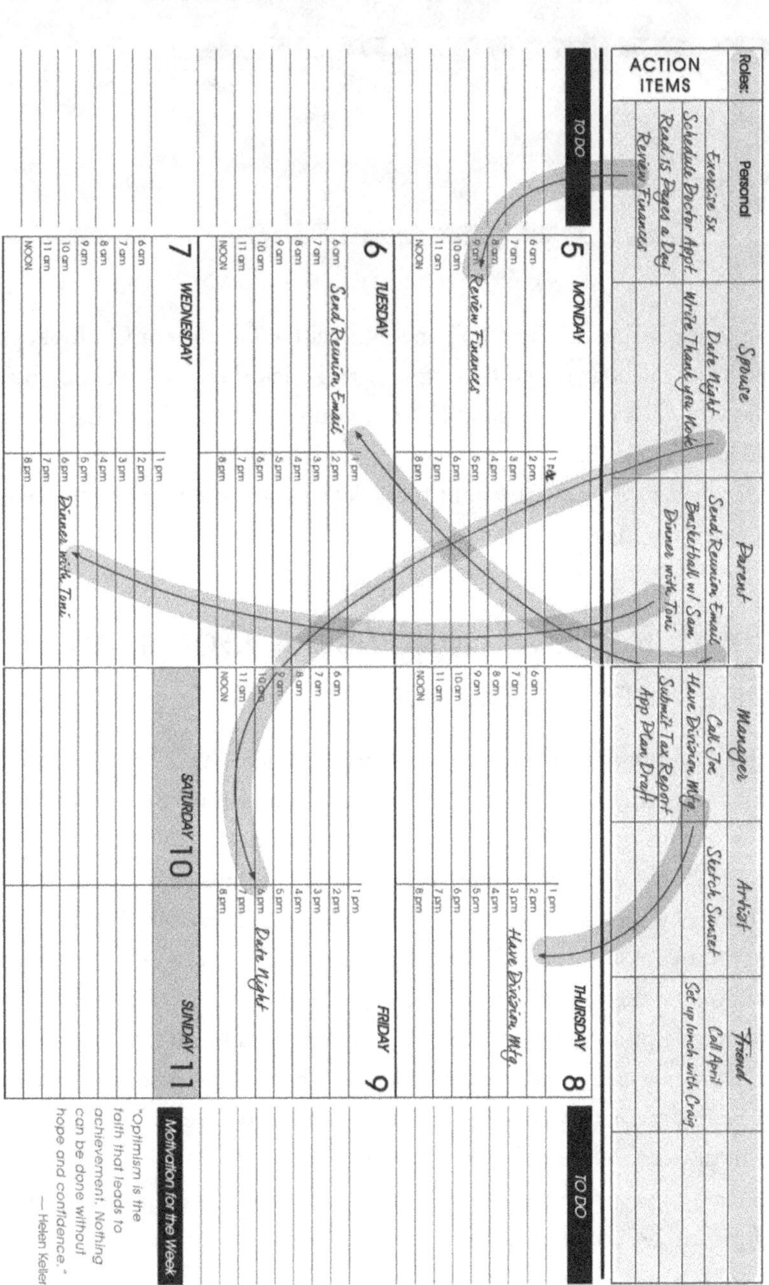

Figure 20. The pre-week planning tool for Chrome and Outlook

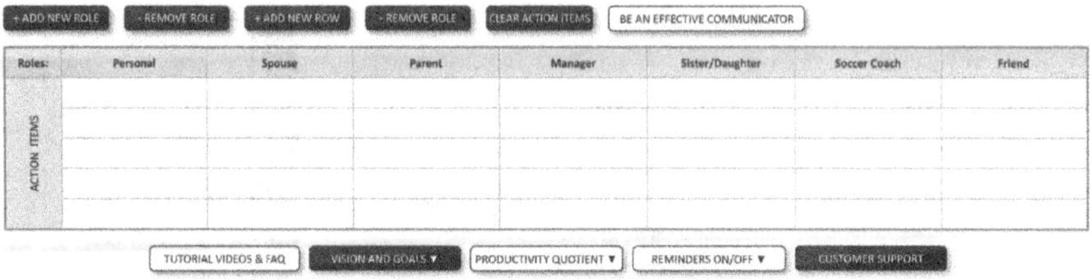

+ ADD NEW ROLE | - REMOVE ROLE | + ADD NEW ROW | - REMOVE ROLE | CLEAR ACTION ITEMS | BE AN EFFECTIVE COMMUNICATOR

Roles:	Personal	Spouse	Parent	Manager	Sister/Daughter	Soccer Coach	Friend
ACTION ITEMS							

TUTORIAL VIDEOS & FAQ | VISION AND GOALS ▼ | PRODUCTIVITY QUOTIENT ▼ | REMINDERS ON/OFF ▼ | CUSTOMER SUPPORT

If you're using the digital planner with either Chrome or Outlook, please open your calendar on your computer and click the blue "expand" button. Once you click on the expand button, you'll see a matrix similar to what's shown in Figure 20.

Now that you have the right tools, let's review the four simple steps for pre-week planning.

Step 1. Review Your Vision, Goals, and Long-Range Calendar

Take a few minutes to review your vision and goals, then ask yourself what you can do this week to move toward accomplishing them. This weekly review means you're looking at them at least once per week—imagine the alignment and focus that comes with being this connected to them.

For some goals, you may not do anything this week. For others, it's important you do specific things during the week. For example, maybe one of your goals in the role of friend is *Average two lunches a month with a friend.* When doing pre-week planning, you may not need to do anything related to that particular goal this week because you have other priorities. However, maybe you're a couple of weeks into the month and haven't scheduled a lunch yet. In that case, it's probably time to prioritize and schedule that lunch.

Can you see from this simple example how pre-week planning can help you prioritize something important to you that otherwise may not happen because of your already busy schedule? Having the goal in the first place is important, but pre-week planning helps you connect the action items to accomplishing the goal. In this particular goal example, you don't need to have lunch with a friend weekly. However, other goals, such as health goals or sales goals, might require you to do something every week. That's why the first part of Step 1 begins with the vision and goals.

Note that your weekly planner has a section in the front where you can write your vision and goals. As mentioned in previous chapters, the planner was designed as a one-stop shop so you can easily and quickly reference your vision and goals each week. If you're using the digital planner, click the Vision and Goals tab to open a drop-down window where you can easily see them while doing pre-week planning.

Pre-week planning is a process that can stand alone and still dramatically increase focus and productivity; however, wouldn't you agree it's way more powerful when aligned with your longer-term vision and goals?

Finally, we recommend briefly reviewing your long-term calendar as part of this step; doing so helps you stay in Q2. For example, the Q2 approach of booking a flight well ahead of time so you get a cheaper airfare and your preferred seat is much better than the Q1 alternative of waiting until the day before your trip, paying for a more expensive ticket, and having limited seating options.

To summarize, Step 1 in pre-week planning is to take a few minutes to review your vision, goals, and long-range calendar so you can stay connected to what you've previously identified as mattering most to you.

Step 2. Write Your Roles

As you did for your vision and goals, identify the five to seven roles that are most important to you. This approach helps you plan your week through the lens of what matters most in each role, which is one of the primary differences between this process and every other approach.

A member of the National Security Agency who attended a Do What Matters Most workshop said the familiar words, "I've planned around my

Figure 21. Writing your roles

Roles:	Personal	Spouse	Parent	Manager	Artist	Friend	

work role my entire career, but I've never thought about planning my week using my roles of mother, wife, and so on. This is so much more than just time management."

Figure 21 shows some potential roles.

If you use our digital or paper planner, write your roles across the top row. You should see the word *roles* on the appropriate row. Notice that the personal role is prewritten for you—this is the most crucial role. In the personal role, you will think about yourself through the lens of what you can do this week to care for yourself physically, mentally, emotionally, and spiritually. In other words, the personal role is all about you taking care of *you* this week. Remember, we can only draw from a well that has water in it. If you want to show up in your other roles, you need to take care of yourself as well.

In Greek, two terms are used to refer to time: *kairos* and *chronos*. Kairos focuses on priorities (roles), and chronos is all about time. Most planners focus only on time (chronos). Pre-week planning brings kairos and chronos together so that you focus on both your priorities and time. Pre-week planning—looking at your week through the lens of your different roles—allows you to lead a life by design, schedule your priorities, and do what matters most. For 96 percent of people, this role-based approach is a big shift because they're looking at more than just their professional role(s).

Step 3. Set Action Items for Each Role

We use the term *weekly action items* rather than weekly goals, but it doesn't really matter what you call them: this step is about having a personal brainstorming session to determine what matters most this week in each of your roles. Imagine how powerful it is to sit down for a few minutes and identify the most important

Figure 22. Set action items for each role

Roles:	Personal	Spouse	Parent	Manager	Artist	Friend	
ACTION ITEMS	Exercise 5x	Date Night	Send Reunion Email	Call Joe	Sketch Sunset	Call April	
	Schedule Doctor Appt	Write Thank you Note	Basketball w/ Sam	Have Division Mtg		Set up lunch with Craig	
	Read 15 Pages a Day		Dinner with Toni	Submit Tax Report			
	Review Finances			App Plan Draft			

actions in each role. Step 3 is the most critical step of pre-week planning and can enhance almost any other planning activity you might already be doing.

Figure 22 shows a sample template with weekly action items for each role, giving you an idea of what this step might look like in both the paper and digital planner formats.

This step moves the majority of your time and focus into Q2. Using the ping-pong balls from the beginning of the book (see Figure 23), you determine what you should put in the aquarium first—that is, what matters most to you in each role.

Figure 23. The ping-pong ball example

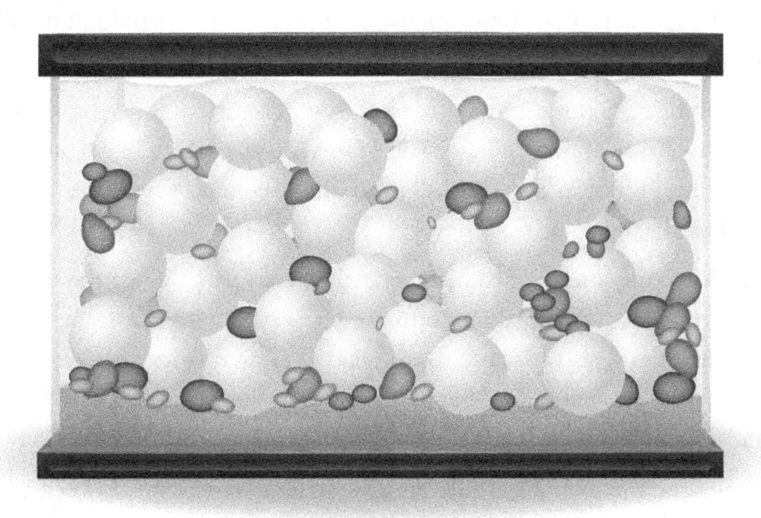

Pre-week planning is dynamic; every week will likely differ from the previous one. Each week, you are also apt to have a different number of action items in each role. Recall the graph from the previous chapter that tracked the average person over five weeks: people consistently see a dramatic increase from week one to week four in the priorities they accomplish. In other words, it's okay to start slowly, with only a couple of action items per role. However, once you do pre-week planning for two or three weeks, you'll probably have additional ideas, and the number of action items you write down in each role will likely increase. This pattern of increasing ideas, plus the practice of thinking specifically about what matters in each role, is why productivity rises when you consistently do pre-week planning.

You don't need a set number of action items per role. Maybe in the role of spouse, you have only two action items this week, but they're two *high-priority* items, such as *having a date night* and *writing a love note*. At the same time, you may consider eight or nine specific action items in your professional role to be high-priority items. Use the Do What Matters Most filter to ask yourself if what you write are Q2 types of activities and reflect the most important things to you.

The following are examples of hypothetical weekly actions by some of the most common roles (these are just examples and you wouldn't do all of these in the same week):

Personal: Run three times, complete two cross-training workouts, do yoga twice, read three chapters of *Start with the Vision*, meditate twice, schedule a physical exam, enroll in an online course, sign up for the September 5k, and so on.

Leader: Take a team member to lunch, finish part one of the strategic plan for our division, do a continue–start–stop with the team, finalize the analytics report for last month, send a birthday note to (a key client), review the purchasing order, schedule one-on-one coaching with (name), and so on.

Spouse or partner: Plan a date night, write a note, send flowers, go on a hike together, make the bed, change the tires, get a new chair that they requested, get the airline tickets for vacation, and so on.

Parent: Have a one-on-one night with (child's name), go on a bike ride, help build a fort, write a note, get ice cream, play basketball, conduct a one-on-one interview, review roles and goals, call (name), and so on.

Keep in mind that these are just common examples to illustrate some action items you might come up with in each respective role. As we already mentioned, you wouldn't be doing all of them in the same week.

You can see that although each of these action items seems simple, they can combine to transform a person's life. Think about when John, the PepsiCo executive, decided to call his son; that seemingly simple action mended a broken relationship and had a generational impact!

The real power of pre-week planning is Step 3. Planning each week through the lens of your roles is a game-changer for most people. This weekly brainstorm you have with yourself—by role—is transformational. This structured approach to planning your week is why your circle of peace and balance will expand, and you'll accomplish an average of 800 to 1,000 additional priorities this year, all with less stress!

Step 4. Schedule a Time for Each Action Item

After you've listed your action items in each role, it's time to make things more concrete by assigning a time to each action item, as shown in Figure 24.

Let's return to the previous friend role example. If you plan to schedule lunch with a friend, figure out a day and time when you will do it this week. Likewise, let's say in the leader role, you plan to meet with one of your team members, finish your strategic plan for your division, call an important client, and conduct a feedback session. When will you do each of these this week?

The point is that rather than keeping these action items as a running to-do list, you assign each action item a time when you plan to do it in the coming week. That simple step significantly increases your likelihood of doing it.

That's it! These are the four simple steps to do pre-week planning effectively: review your vision/goals, identify your roles, determine what matters most in each role this week, and assign a time to each action item.

Figure 24. Schedule a time for each action item

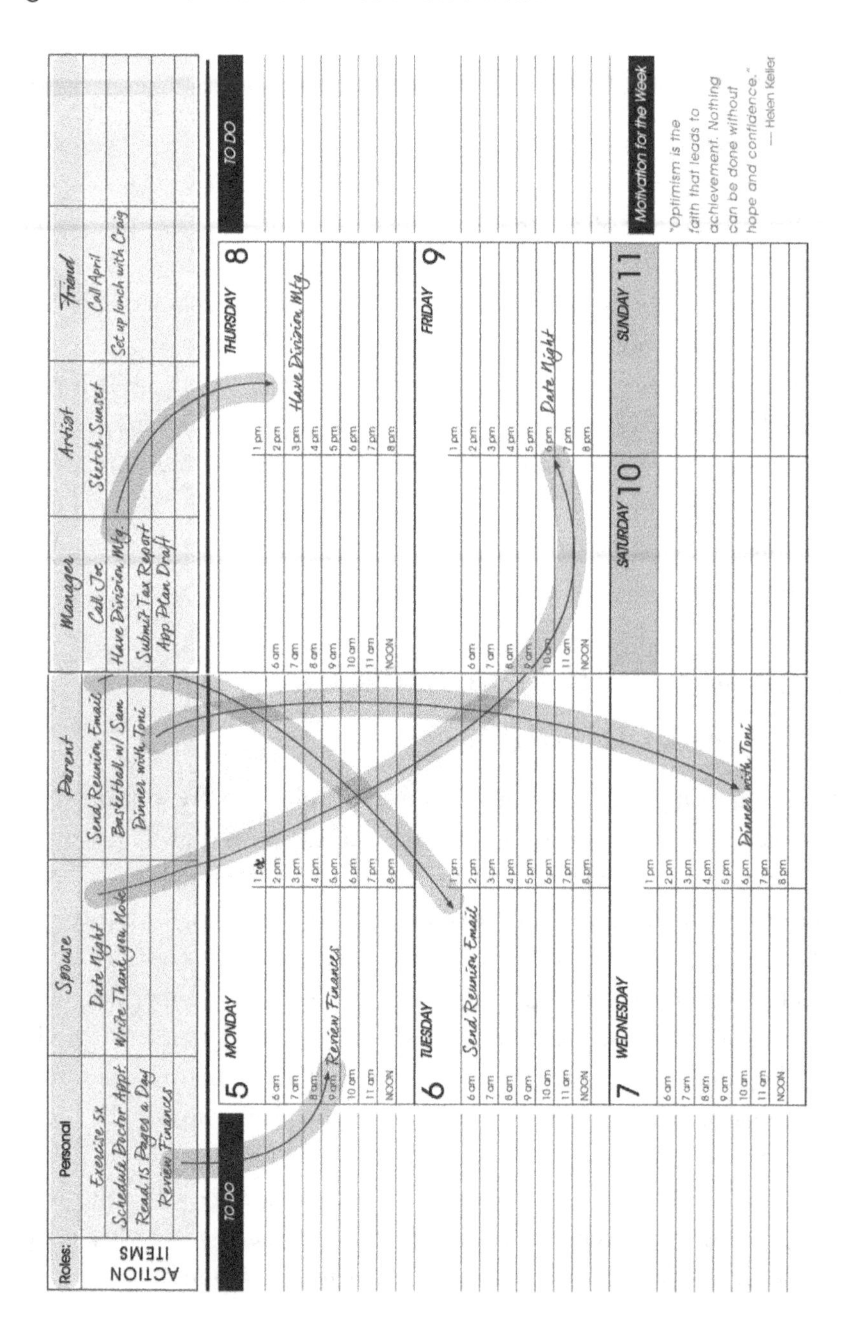

There are hundreds of variations you could incorporate into pre-week planning, but it's important to keep these four steps as the core process. These steps and the tools supporting them are what differentiate this structured approach from every other planning process.

The Productivity Quotient

We briefly mentioned the *productivity quotient* in the previous chapter as a way to track your progress. Doing so is optional, but we recommend tracking it for a handful of weeks until you are consistent—that's exactly what we do with our coaching clients. Some of the paper planners and the digital planner include a box titled Productivity Quotient (PQ). To determine your PQ, divide your planned action items by the total number you accomplished that week. Ideally, a PQ is in the 70 to 80 percent range. If it dips below 70 percent, you need to investigate why. Are you overscheduling, not leaving room for Q1 flexibility, or procrastinating? The reason the target isn't 100 percent is because we know life happens, and no week ever goes exactly as planned. Aiming for 70 to 80 percent builds grace into your calendar, and that's the PQ range all the research from the previous chapter assumes.

Take Action

A surgeon who's been doing pre-week planning for years said, "Pre-week planning is simple, yet it takes effort to do each weekend. But it's so worth it!" Will pre-week planning require some effort? Sure! But, as our friend said, it's so worth it.

Pre-week planning is a habit and takes discipline; it requires about 20 to 45 minutes each week. Our surgeon friend told us that during the weeks he does pre-week planning, he's highly productive. When he doesn't do it, he feels more stressed, and a lot of things tend to slip through the cracks and not get done. Almost all of those who develop this habit would say the same thing.

Anytime you develop a new habit, it will require effort, even when the habit itself is a game-changer. Developing a new habit takes discipline, which we define as *doing the right thing at the right time, regardless of how we feel about it.*

The best time to take action and start pre-week planning is right now—this week! We invite you to pause what you're doing and plan for the remainder of this week. Pull out a sheet of paper or your planner, write down your roles, brainstorm your priorities by role for the remainder of this week, and schedule a time for each one. Please go through the four steps to experience how simple and powerful this process is.

Then, choose a time this weekend when you'll most likely have some quiet time to do your pre-week planning for the next week. If you haven't already done it, consider setting a reminder to do pre-week planning. In other words, plan a time to do it. Some people find it helpful to treat pre-week planning as an ongoing process throughout the weekend. For example, they start on Friday afternoon before they leave work and add other actions or ideas to their roles throughout the weekend as they think of them. Ultimately, you can do whatever works best for you.

Dorene, the COO of Discover Healing, treats pre-week planning as an ongoing process throughout the weekend and says this about her approach:

> I often hear employees speak about the dread of Monday, and I, too, have considered that at different times. You know the lyrics: "Monday, Monday, can't trust that day. Monday, Monday, sometimes it just turns out that way."
>
> There is an answer to those Monday morning blues. It's called pre-week planning. How refreshing not to have to think about or decide what you have to do first thing Monday morning. With pre-week planning, your week is laid out in front of you, and you know exactly your direction.
>
> I have used pre-week planning for years. On Friday afternoon, I start to plan my next week. Using my planner, I place all my meetings that are recurring for each week. I also arrange any other meetings I know I need to have so that the times are set and coordinated. I take the time to think through the various items I need to accomplish based on my different roles and place those in my plan.
>
> This provides a great start to a great week. My mind doesn't feel overwhelmed because I've already thought through these items and know there is a time for each one.

With pre-week planning, I can think, *Monday, Monday, so good to me. Monday mornin', it was all I hoped it would be.*

Dorene exemplifies the peace, calm, and focus that come with pre-week planning—no matter what may show up during the week. She's going into her week ready for Q1 because she's already prioritized her Q2 actions, or what matters most to her.

Now that you've seen how well this process works for Dorene, there's another valuable angle to be aware of—sharing your week with your partner or spouse if that applies to you. Frustration is one of the primary reasons for divorce or for team members to leave an organization. If you think about the root cause of frustration, it typically stems from misaligned expectations. A team member thinks the leader should be doing *Y*, and the leader thinks the team member should be doing *X*. When those expectations aren't aligned, frustration results. The same idea is true in relationships. Pre-week planning can help you avoid the inevitable conflicts of Q1, such as, "I thought *you* were going to take her to soccer!" When you sit down with your partner (hopefully after you have both individually done your pre-week planning) and align your priorities for the week, it ensures you are going in the same direction and focused jointly on what matters most. Most importantly, it aligns expectations and gives clarity to the week.

Likewise, that's why, in the previous chapter, we recommended that teams hold a weekly alignment meeting at the beginning of the week. The hope is that each team member will come to the meeting already having done their pre-week planning. Imagine the alignment and focus on a team when each person does pre-week planning, and then they meet to align around what matters most that week!

That said, now is the best time to take action. Figure out when you will have a quiet 20 to 45 minutes and schedule that time for pre-week planning.

Digital Planner Tips

Everyone has their preferences about what tool they'll use when doing pre-week planning; some people prefer paper, others digital formats, and some a hybrid approach. This topic is important enough that we'll take a couple of

Figure 25. The digital planner for Chrome or Outlook

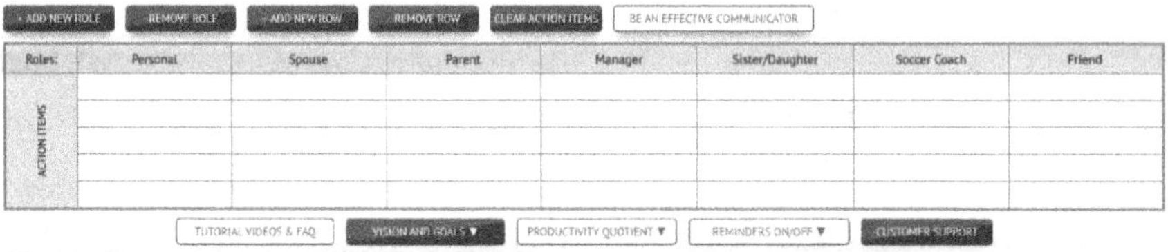

+ ADD NEW ROLE | REMOVE ROLE | ADD NEW ROW | REMOVE ROW | CLEAR ACTION ITEMS | BE AN EFFECTIVE COMMUNICATOR

Roles:	Personal	Spouse	Parent	Manager	Sister/Daughter	Soccer Coach	Friend
ACTION ITEMS							

TUTORIAL VIDEOS & FAQ | VISION AND GOALS ▼ | PRODUCTIVITY QUOTIENT ▼ | REMINDERS ON/OFF ▼ | CUSTOMER SUPPORT

minutes to share some digital planner tips for those going that route. If you'd like to use the digital planner and have already installed it on your Outlook or Chrome calendar, please open it now so you can follow along. If not, and you'd like to use it, you can get it at DoWhatMattersMostPlanner.com. Figure 25 shows the digital planner page on Chrome or Outlook.

If you love the paper planner and don't plan to use the digital version, feel free to skim the next couple of pages. Otherwise, here are our tips for making the most of the digital experience:

- **Get daily reminders and quotes.** You can select the "Reminders on/off" button and choose to get motivational quotes and pre-week planning reminders. These are helpful when you need a little pick-me-up or motivation boost in the middle of the day.
- **Set the default event time in Chrome or Outlook to no more than 30 minutes.** If the default is longer, your online calendar will likely be cluttered and unreadable.
- **Share your vision and goals.** The Vision and Goals tab has the option to email your vision and goals to others. Consider emailing them to yourself as a backup. As noted in earlier chapters, sharing your vision and goals is a powerful accountability tip.
- **Start pre-week planning by using the Clear Action Items button.** In a paper planner, every time you turn the page to a new week, you get a blank page . . . meaning it's a fresh start. Likewise, pressing the Clear Action Items button in the digital planner will clear your action

items and give you a fresh start each week. This is important because it forces you to ask what matters most this week in each role. It fosters creativity when you need to start anew with each role, so that you're not tempted to complacently repeat the same thing each week.

- **Use the weekly view from about 6 a.m. to 10 p.m.** If you're using Google Calendar, you can use CTRL + or - to zoom in and out until you can see the appropriate weekly view. This works on almost any screen size. However, Outlook only lets you zoom out so far, so using a larger monitor rather than a laptop is a better option. That way, you can see the entire week from morning until evening.
- **Click and click versus drag and drop.** This is a critical step. Please watch the short tutorial video when you add the planner to your Chrome or Outlook calendar. For the Chrome calendar, you'll need to left-click on the action item box, then left-click on the time you want to do it during the week to create the calendar event and sync it with all your devices. For Outlook, you left-click on the action item and drag it to the appropriate time during the week to create the event and sync with all your Outlook calendars. Once you've done this a few times, it's easy and takes only a few seconds.
- **Add roles or rows.** Click the appropriate button in the upper left-hand corner to add or delete role columns. You can also add more rows if you need more action items than the default space allows.
- **Avoid relying on artificial intelligence (AI).** There are all kinds of new AI planning tools; we're even incorporating AI to help people customize their own planner. We'll also use it in our training to help people with their vision, goals, and pre-week planning. However, while AI might be helpful in some ways, you can't fully delegate pre-week planning to anyone, including AI. This process encourages you to use your intuition and inspiration to identify what matters most in each role this week. For example, in the role of parent, maybe you took a family trip earlier in the year to Yosemite National Park so this week, your action item is *Start on the Yosemite picture book*. AI

could never generate an idea like that—only you could. Although AI might be a help or support, it can never fully replace you.

- **Select a principle of the week to focus on.** The box labeled Principle of the Week comes from our other leadership training focused on the 12 Principles of Highly Successful Leaders. As part of that training, we invite people and teams to focus on one principle a week and then repeat the process every 12 weeks. That box lets you select which principle you want to focus on this week. If you'd like to focus on something besides one of the 12 principles, you have the option to type in your own focus area each week.
- **Use your desktop computer or laptop, not a mobile device.** As a reminder, the screen size on a tablet or phone isn't big enough to do pre-week planning. In addition, Chrome extensions and plug-ins don't work on phones and tablets, so until they do, you need to do your pre-week planning on a laptop or desktop computer. The larger your screen size, the simpler it is to do pre-week planning because you can easily pull up the weekly view and the planning tool.
- **Watch the tutorial videos and contact support with any questions.** We want you to be set up for success and love your digital planner. Before you start using it, please click the Tutorial videos and FAQ button and take a few minutes to watch the videos. Likewise, if you still have a question, click the Customer Support button, and our team will help answer any questions.

If you want to use the digital planner, these tips will give you a great start and help you fully leverage the tool.

Pre-week Planning Is a Game-Changer!

Regardless of what tool you use to do pre-week planning, you've probably noticed by now that it's a personal and professional game-changer. From the professional side, when a team member does pre-week planning, it translates into better leadership, a higher-producing person or team, higher profitability, a better workplace environment, a more aligned team, increased sales, an improved culture, and a more engaged workforce. On the personal side, it translates into improved health, better relationships, internal alignment, increased balance, and a more profound sense of peace and focus.

We love stories because they show us that anyone can do this. Stories suddenly make everything relatable, spark new ideas, and give people the confidence and enthusiasm to commit to pre-week planning. In that same spirit, we would like to share a few brief stories about how pre-week planning has helped ordinary people do seemingly small things that have led to extraordinary results.

Our first story is about Christine. She told us she meant to take her daughter on a special mommy/daughter date to celebrate her birthday in September. She told us this story in March and still hadn't taken her daughter on that date—six months after her birthday! Christine commented that time had slipped away from her, and she'd been "too busy."

She obviously didn't feel good about missing the birthday date, so she was thrilled to learn about pre-week planning. Christine was searching for something to help her prioritize her time and escape the monotonous grind. She was confident this would be the answer to help her take control of her schedule so that this kind of missed opportunity wouldn't happen again.

After just three weeks of pre-week planning, she sent a message saying, "I love this! It's the first time I don't feel stressed, and I'm accomplishing more than I ever thought possible. It's relatively easy, and it has made a huge difference. You will be happy to know that I took my daughter on the long-overdue mommy/daughter date, which was awesome. *Thank you, thank you!*"

How many times have you felt like Christine? In other words, how often do you feel like your priorities are slipping through the cracks or not getting done? In Christine's case, pre-week planning helped her make the time to do what had eluded her for months. How important do you think that date was to her daughter, and what's the impact of that memory they made together?

In another case, we were in Kigali, Rwanda, for a Do What Matters Most workshop. Several hundred Rwandans participated—some were college students, and others were successful business leaders. It was an incredible experience for us to be there with such an extraordinary group of people.

Twenty-five years before this workshop, this country experienced a terrible genocide in which more than one million Rwandans were killed.

During our visit, we had the chance to meet privately with the president of Rwanda and hear about the incredible transformation the country has experienced since the genocide. It has transformed into a country of opportunity. At the time of this writing, it is the fifth safest country in the world and the second fastest-growing economy in all of Africa, and there has been an unprecedented alignment within the country. Needless to say, it is an extraordinary place, and it was a privilege to be there.

The attendees at our conference were from a wide range of experience and backgrounds. Among those who attended was a young manager in his 20s named Samuel Yesashimwe. He stood out to us as someone who was serious and would do whatever it took to succeed. Several months after we met in Rwanda, Samuel wrote us an email and said the following:

> Learning about the Do What Matters Most program of vision, goals, and pre-week planning was a life-changing experience. I am usually organized, but since I learned about the big three, I have taken it to the next level. I finished my vision and goals and consistently do pre-week planning. It has increased my productivity by at least 30 percent, and the results are incredible. In April, I was promoted and led the IBM CSC Program in Rwanda. Because it was new and there was so much to do, I probably would have failed without the excellent planning and management skills and tools.
>
> On a personal level, one of the exercises during the conference was to develop our roles and goals for the year. I had always wanted to attend graduate school in another country but didn't think it could happen to me. I considered three schools: Stanford, Oklahoma Christian University, and London Graduate School of Business.
>
> I would like to tell you that *today is my first day in the MBA program at Oklahoma Christian University.*
>
> There is so much that happened when I applied these tools. May God bless you!

When we received this email from Samuel, we were elated for him.

Samuel had known he wanted to attend an international university for years, but he never did anything about it. We've all procrastinated and put off things we knew were important; likewise, Samuel kept pushing these important ideas back month after month and year after year. When he focused on the big three, he finally took action. He developed a goal to send applications to all three schools by October 1st. As part of pre-week planning, he did something toward accomplishing that goal most weeks. For example, one week, he collected letters of recommendation; the next, he wrote the required essay letters; and the next, he had someone review his applications. The combination of vision, goals, and pre-week planning helped Samuel focus on what mattered most and finally take action to go after it. His vision was clear, he had specific goals to realize his vision, and pre-week planning helped him stay ahead of the curve—in Q2—to achieve the goals.

We will share one final example that is personal to us. Steve has been doing pre-week planning for almost 45 years, and Rob has been doing it for about 28 years. Just as it has been life-changing for thousands of others, it has also been life-changing for us. In fact, we would go as far as to say that without our vision, goals, and pre-week planning, our lives would be total chaos.

A few years ago, Rob flew to Indianapolis to give a keynote speech to 300 entrepreneurs and business leaders. During his pre-week planning that week, Rob wrote in the role of father, *Write a note to Lana.* Every week, he comes up with something to do for or with his kids, and for Lana this week, it was to write her a note.

It was a beautiful blue-sky morning, and Lana had just walked out the door to school. Rob quickly took a minute to write her a note telling her how much he loved her and left it on her bed, then got in his car and left for the airport.

The next evening, Rob was getting on the plane to fly home. It was already late, and he wouldn't get home until around midnight. Rob had just sat down when his phone buzzed, and he saw an incoming text from his wife. He pulled out his phone and read the text. "I know you'll get home late and the house will be dark, so I don't want you to miss this special note from Lana. She snuck into our room and left it on our headboard." (See Figure 26.)

Figure 26. Lana's note

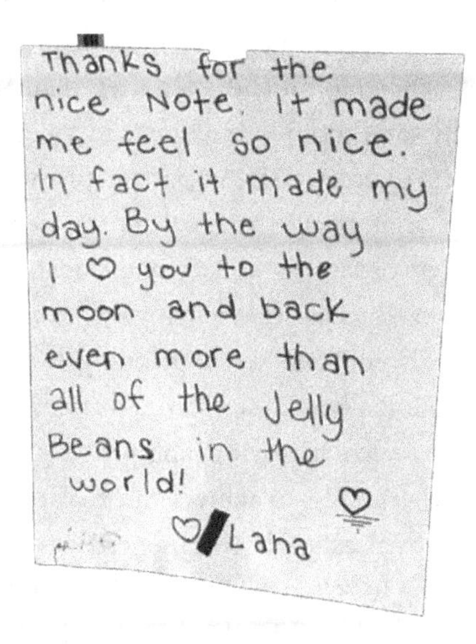

Thanks for the
nice Note. It made
me feel so nice.
In fact it made my
day. By the way
I ♡ you to the
moon and back
even more than
all of the Jelly
Beans in the
world!
♡ Lana

It was a special moment for Rob, and a tear slid gently down his cheek. He thanked his wife for the text and put away his phone. No matter what great things had happened that day, none of them topped this note from his daughter.

This back-and-forth note exchange continued for several weeks and became a fun game for them.

We share this because it took Rob less than one minute to write that note to Lana. The short, meaningful note exchange created some great memories. Would Rob have written this note without pre-week planning? Probably not!

How many opportunities are there to do seemingly small things? More importantly, what is the long-term impact of doing those seemingly small things, such as exercising, doing something to care for your mental and emotional health, having a date night, writing a note, maintaining a friendship, or having lunch with a client?

We are all far from perfect, which is all the more reason why everyone will benefit so much from vision, goals, and pre-week planning. These three habits help anyone focus on what matters most and proactively schedule their priorities.

Wrap Up

Nobody has told us, "Pre-week planning didn't really work for me." Instead, people are constantly sharing stories about how pre-week planning shifted their focus and helped them accomplish things they had been thinking about for years, just like Christine, John, Amy, and many others from previous chapters.

We continue to use the term *life-changing* because we believe pre-week planning is exactly that. How can pre-week planning not be life-changing when it involves sitting down every week to review your vision and goals, listing what matters most in each role this week, and assigning a time to each item? With this approach, it's easy to see how you can accomplish so many more priorities throughout the week. To take the macro view, it's all of these seemingly small action items that will ultimately make up your dash.

Pre-week planning is a habit that takes discipline and consistency—doing it week after week, even when you may not feel like it. When you're consistent, the rewards are worth it. At the same time, give yourself some grace. If you miss a week or even two, it's okay. Pick up where you left off and start again. For some, this will be an easier habit to develop than for others. Don't compare yourself to others; focus on your own journey.

Some people comment weeks after the training that they thought about their weeks through the lens of their various roles, but they didn't actually do pre-week planning. Those same people often say that even the shift in thinking was life-changing. However, those who later do pre-week planning using either the paper or digital planner notice a huge jump in what they accomplish versus just thinking about it. So, this is your journey, and the best time to start is right now!

Remember, pre-week planning takes only around 30 minutes. So, less than 1 percent of your week will determine what you do with the other 99 percent of your week.

Imagine how great it would feel to enjoy your work; be a better contributor; have improved health, relationships, and finances; experience less stress; and have a strong sense of purpose and direction. Imagine the team dynamic and how great it would be to have an aligned team focused on Q2 activities, increased productivity, and a fun culture.

At the beginning of the book, we said doing what matters most is both a *mindset* and a *skillset*. Vision, goals, and pre-week planning are the skillset. The mindset is having the willingness and discipline to apply the skillset consistently.

In the past six chapters, we've shared the skillset and how to apply it. In the final chapters, we'll share some ideas on why time is our most valuable resource and why developing these habits is so important to start now.

REFLECTION QUESTIONS FOR THIS CHAPTER

1. How do you feel pre-week planning can help you prioritize your time and do what matters most?
2. Who else do you know that would benefit from doing pre-week planning (child, partner, team member)? Why would pre-week planning be helpful to them?
3. When do you think is the best time for you to do pre-week planning each week? Have you set an alarm or reminder?
4. Is there someone you would feel comfortable having as an accountability partner to join you in pre-week planning (coworker, partner, etc.)?

10

Time and Habits—Make Each Day Count!

Time is the great equalizer because it is the universal resource—we all have access to it and the same amount of it. What a person does with that time determines their legacy and dash.

We want to share a great story we once heard to show how precious it is to use our time wisely because once it's gone, it's gone. Since we first heard this story, we've found different versions of it, but the principle is what's important.

••••

One evening, a father was trying to finish several projects with looming deadlines. He had already missed dinner and knew he would work late into the night. He sat at the kitchen table in the dimly lit kitchen, sorting through the different charts on his laptop.

His young son approached him and quietly asked his father, "Dad, how much do you make in an hour?" The father felt his frustration start to rise, adding to the stress he already felt from the looming deadlines. This question wasn't the conversation he wanted to have when he was so focused. He tersely told his young son, "I make about $40 an hour, but that isn't your business." The son paused and asked his father, "Dad, can I borrow $20?" The dad's patience was gone; he thought his son would waste the money on something and felt like this conversation was eating up his valuable time. He raised his voice and told his son, "No, I'm not giving you $20; now go to your room!" The dejected young boy lowered his head and quietly walked to his bedroom. The father sat in his chair, frustrated and tired. The more he thought about it, the angrier he became.

After about 30 minutes, the father began to calm down, and he realized that he had taken his work frustration out on his young son. His heart softened, realizing he had been too hard on him. He got up from the table and walked to his son's bedroom. He could hear his son quietly crying as he approached the bedroom, causing his heart to sink even further.

He gently approached his son and sat beside him on his bed. He told his son, "I'm sorry I was so hard on you. It's been a long day, and I took out some of my frustrations on you. You must have had a good reason for wanting the $20. If you need $20, I can give you the $20." His father then handed his son a $20 bill.

His son instantly smiled and wiped away his tears. He sat up in bed and reached over to his bedstand. He excitedly grabbed several more dollar bills that had been sitting there. He quickly counted the money, including the new $20 addition, and saw that he had more than $50. With a big smile, the boy said to his dad, "Dad, I didn't have enough money before, but now I do." He then asked, "Now that I have $40, can I buy an hour of your time so we can play together?"

The father was ashamed. His heart sank. He put his arms around his son, feeling his own tears streak down his cheeks as he realized how important this moment was.

••••

When we first heard this story, it touched us. It reminded us that time is fleeting, and the time to do what matters most is now—tomorrow isn't guaranteed for anyone. We all have the same amount of time available in a day, and as already mentioned, once it is gone, it is gone. It is important to be aware of the destination or vision while still living in the present and enjoying the journey. When people are at work, they should be fully present and engaged, doing what matters most. Then, when they go home, they should be fully present with their partner, children, and even with themselves. Although nobody can be "on" 100 percent of the time, vision, goals, and pre-week planning help them accomplish *a lot* more than they likely would otherwise, both at home and at work.

Life is filled with ups and downs, as well as unplanned surprises. Because we cannot predict the future, developing our vision and goals and being consistent with pre-week planning helps us navigate life during the highs and lows.

Even when someone does everything right, unexpected challenges will still pop up. When you have a clear vision and goals and are consistent with pre-week planning, you will almost always be in a much better position to handle whatever comes your way than someone who doesn't have this foundation.

For example, we have a dear friend and coaching client—we'll call him Nathan—who is an executive of a large, nationally recognized bank. One day, while driving with his wife to their cabin, his tire unexpectedly blew out, he lost control, and their SUV rolled several times. Tragically, his wife sustained a head injury and ended up in a coma for nearly 18 months.

Nathan spent many sleepless nights during those 18 months thinking about his life, work, and family. No one would wish for this type of accident, yet Nathan knew he couldn't go back and change time; he accepted that it did happen and could happen to anyone. Nearly everything in his life was going great before the accident. However, by the end of that tragic day, his life had flipped upside down.

During this challenging time, Nathan was still an executive at the bank, a father to several adult children, and a grandparent to numerous grandchildren. He still needed to "show up" and be there for his team, his family, and even himself. When he returned to his vision, goals, and pre-week planning, that was what helped him juggle it all and kept him from going to a dark place.

During this time, Nathan made a concerted effort to stay focused on his vision (his purpose), goals, and what mattered most each week. He used his time to focus on what he could control rather than on what he couldn't. He visited his wife every day in the hospital to talk with her and caress her hand; even though she could not respond, he stayed connected. He spent time with his children, was a more committed leader at the bank, and took a more profound interest in his team and clients. This grueling period was a time of deep introspection for Nathan. After 18 months and many consultations with the doctors, the family finally made the agonizing decision to end her life support.

Nathan's vision, goals, and pre-week planning took an ugly situation nobody would ever wish for and helped him make the best of it. He believes there is a higher power, and he used this experience to become a better version of himself—a better leader, father, grandfather, and community member. The people on Nathan's team expressed that he is one of the best leaders they have ever worked with throughout their careers, and this experience made him an even better leader than he already was.

As with Nathan, no matter what may come your way, when you have the big three, you are in a stronger position to handle whatever is thrown at you—big or small. These three habits give you a reason to get up every morning; they give your heart a reason to keep beating. They help you stay attuned to what you can control instead of worrying about what you cannot. They help you be one of the best contributors to your team. And finally, they help you focus on what matters most with the precious time you have.

Habits

Because of the compounding effect discussed earlier in the book, you'll notice that when you start planning your weeks through the lens of your different roles, multiple areas of your life will start improving simultaneously. You'll see an immediate impact on what you do with your time, personally and professionally.

To illustrate that point, a friend once said, "Health is wealth." When people prioritize their health and feel healthy, they're in a better position to build relationships with family, friends, and coworkers. When their health and relationships are good, they're much more likely to be focused while working. It's the compounding effect in action. When one area improves, other areas seem to start improving as well. This is why the circle of peace and balance expands in all directions when someone is consistent with the Do What Matters Most habits.

One of the most critical personal commitments is to make pre-week planning a habit. Pre-week planning aligns your actions with your vision and goals, so the hope and objective is that it becomes a habit for the rest of your life. Remember, if you miss a week or two, that's okay; just get back on the horse and start again. We've all done the same with different parts of our lives.

Sometimes people tell us, "You know, I loved pre-week planning, but I got out of the habit for some reason. When I did it, my life was so much better." If you once had the habit of doing it and, for some reason, stopped, this is your time to start again. It doesn't matter if weeks or months have passed; you can restart today. The more you develop and maintain the habit, the more you'll experience a positive impact in every area of your life!

Knowing that pre-week planning is a habit, we want to share a powerful poem illustrating the importance of choosing carefully which habits to nurture and develop:

I am your constant companion.
I am your greatest helper or your heaviest burden.
I will push you onward or drag you down to failure.
I am completely at your command.
Half the things you do, you might just as well turn over to me,
and I will do them quickly and correctly.
I am easily managed; but, you must be firm with me.
Show me exactly how you want something done, and after a few lessons
I will do it automatically.
I am the servant of all great people.
And, alas, of all failures as well.
Those who are great, I have made great.
Those who are failures, I have made failures.
I am not a machine, though I work with the precision of a machine.
Plus, the intelligence of a person.
You may run me for profit or run me for ruin; it makes no difference to me.
Take me, train me, be firm with me, and I will place the world at your feet.

Be easy with me, and I will destroy you.
Who am I?

I AM HABIT!

Isn't that a great poem? It encourages us to examine our habits and ask whether they are moving us toward our vision or away from it.

Most of us have areas of our lives we want to improve, whether making more money, earning a promotion, improving a specific relationship, or achieving better health. Our daily habits usually determine how we do in each area. Rarely will something magically change; it takes time and focus. If you want to improve an area of your life, the habit of pre-week planning will help you make the time to focus on those areas.

In other words, we need to develop habits that lead to achieving our vision and goals.

Our research has found six primary areas people are concerned with and think about often when it comes to happiness and satisfaction, many of which will likely resonate with you as well:

1. Health and well-being (this was easily the #1 answer)
2. Relationships
3. Money
4. Connecting with a purpose
5. Doing something they enjoy
6. Job performance

Why share that research in this chapter where we're talking about time and habits? The reason is that you're now familiar with the Do What Matters Most program and the structured approach of vision, goals, and pre-week planning. In that context, consider the impact of your vision, goals, and pre-week planning on those six areas. How will vision and goals, and especially pre-week planning, affect your physical and mental health? How about your relationships with your family, friends, and coworkers? How about your purpose or what you do with your time at work? The point is that if you maintain the habit of pre-week planning, these six areas will be positively impacted for the rest of your life!

Steve's business partner, Dave, commented that of all the things he's learned in business over the course of decades, pre-week planning is probably the most valuable tool and skill. Everything he does, personally and professionally, flows through and results from pre-week planning.

The habits you work to develop in the coming weeks, months, and years—especially the habit of pre-week planning—will ultimately help you achieve what you want to accomplish. If someone wants to improve something in their life, they usually need to adjust or develop a corresponding habit. In some cases, that means developing new and helpful habits; in others, it means changing old and unhelpful ones. In other words, your habits move you either toward or away from your vision and goals. Ultimately, your vision, goals, and pre-week planning are the habits that help you achieve your desired outcome.

Think about the impact the Do What Matters Most habits had on our CEO friend from South Africa, who laid down his last pack of cigarettes; the sales team that went from averaging 17 to 34 sales a day; John, the PepsiCo executive who rekindled a relationship with his son; Deanna, who went from being a task-saturated commercial real estate agent to taking control of her life and schedule; or Christine, who finally took her daughter on the long-awaited mommy/daughter date. You get the idea. Vision, goals, and pre-week planning are about creating high-performance habits that align your time and energy with what matters most.

Supercharged Productivity Tips

When we decided to write this book, we purposefully chose to focus on the structured approach of vision, goals, and pre-week planning. After all, this approach is new for 96 percent of people. Although the entire focus of the book has been on the big three, we also want to share a handful of important productivity tips. Based on the other findings in our research, we felt these tips would be helpful to include because you can implement them in conjunction with the big three. Remember, these additional tips are just that: tips. We want the focus to stay on the big three, but we believe a brief summary of these five tips will also increase your productivity and help maximize your time.

1. Do the Becoming Your Best morning routine.

The morning sets the tone for the day, and the day usually goes better when we get off to a strong start. Another term for your morning routine is the *power hour*. The idea is to schedule between 15 minutes and 1 hour in the morning to take care of yourself; the time varies depending on the day. When you do pre-week planning, you can be intentional about your power hour or morning routine.

Here are some suggestions for things you might schedule as part of your morning power hour (to be clear, we're not suggesting you do all of them every day; instead, choose what matters most and plan them into your week as part of your pre-week planning):

- Drink 16+ ounces of water each morning when you wake up.
- Make your bed.
- Stretch; take a few minutes for some form of yoga or meditation.
- Exercise.
- Meditate.
- Pray.
- Read.
- Ask yourself what you can do to make it a great day.
- Focus on your vision or positive affirmations for three to four minutes before you roll out of bed. What will you do today to make them a reality?
- Review the key actions and calendar for the day. Identify the top one or two priorities.

Again, this is just a sample of ideas for your morning routine. When possible, *do not* look at your phone or email for the first 30 minutes of the day.

Use the power hour and develop a routine to focus on yourself and your personal role. You'll usually have more energy throughout the day when you take care of yourself first.

2. Prioritize sleep, exercise, and a healthy diet.

There are countless books written about each one of these. Suffice it to say that someone who sleeps well, makes time to exercise, and is mindful about the food they eat will likely perform and produce at a higher level than someone who doesn't. These three things also contribute to longevity and increased happiness. If you have not incorporated aspects of sleep, exercise, and diet into your vision and goals, we highly recommend you consider doing so.

Our bodies are like jets. You cannot put water into a jet's fuel tank and expect it to perform well—a jet needs jet fuel. Likewise, our bodies need "fuel" to perform well, which often comes from sleep, exercise, and food. Seems so simple, right? If these were automatic, many of the problems plaguing us and our society wouldn't exist.

One of the keys to getting the right amount of sleep, exercise, and a proper diet is what you intentionally plan into your week during pre-week planning.

3. Chairfly your day.

You're probably wondering what *chairfly* means. The most successful pilots are those who chairfly the important parts of their mission before they fly it. In other words, before they walk out to the jet, the pilots *visualize* the most critical aspects of the upcoming flight in their mind's eye. In the calm of the briefing room, they mentally walk through (visualize) the busiest, most intense parts of their flight *before* they get in their jets and execute it in the air.

Likewise, we invite you to take a few minutes in the morning to chairfly your day. First, sit down and review your calendar. Review what you scheduled for the day as part of your pre-week planning and identify the two or three highest priorities. When possible, it often helps to schedule the highest-priority items in the morning when your energy level is high. We recognize this isn't always possible, but when you can, the morning is usually the ideal time to get things done.

Once you identify the two or three priorities for the day, you can calmly close your eyes and chairfly your day. Mentally walk through it and get prepared for what might show up unannounced. This way, if a Q1 item pops up, you know your priorities and how you might shift things around.

Instead of just jumping into the day and hoping for the best, take a few minutes to chairfly—you will feel calmer, more focused, and at peace with your day.

4. Improve your workstation with multiple monitors.

You can accomplish a lot with just one monitor, but two or more monitors will allow you to accomplish the same task in a fraction of the time. In the *New York Times* report of a Jon Peddie Research survey, dual monitors increased productivity by up to 46 percent.[1]

You can find the number of monitors that works best for you. Everyone we've talked with agrees that multiple monitors or a larger screen will allow you to get work done more effectively and efficiently.

5. Learn to say no.

If a coworker or peer continually asks you to do things that put you in Q1 or Q3, it almost always negatively impacts your productivity. Saying no the right way benefits the entire team. For example, if a supervisor asks you to take care of a project while you're in the middle of another project, it is crucial to base your decision on what is best for you, your boss, and the organization. One example of a good response is to say, "Yes, I can work on this new project, but I'll need to stop working on (the old one) to finish it. That means I won't be able to have X done by the time I promised. Would you prefer I finish the other project on time or work on this new project?" This puts the ball in the supervisor's court and is often received very well. It aligns expectations and helps the supervisor understand what you're already working on. If the new project is more important, the supervisor will likely be okay with the other project being late. If the other project being on time is more important, then you're both aware of that.

Since you've done your pre-week planning, you've already identified what is most important that week. If someone or something encroaches on your time, you can pause and ask yourself, *Is this what matters most?* It may be best to say no if it doesn't align with your vision, goals, and pre-week planning. The main point here is that you have developed the skill to identify what matters most to you personally and professionally. Apply that skill to decide whether to say yes or no.

The ability to say no is undoubtedly an art. The whole point of this book is to help you do what matters most. Sometimes that means you'll need to unload certain commitments so you can use your time to refocus on your priorities.

Wrap Up

Time is our most valuable resource. Life is about the journey as much as it is about the destination. The reason for having a vision, establishing roles and goals, and doing pre-week planning is to learn to live in the present while having an eye on the future. Ultimately, what you do with your time will form your habits, and your habits will define your legacy. The vision is your internal compass, the roles and goals are your annual targets, and pre-week planning is about living in the present to make each day count!

The big three are life-changing habits because they determine what we do with our time and what other habits we cultivate and develop. As with any other habit, ingraining them will require discipline and focus. We invite you to commit internally and join us in making the big three lifelong habits.

W. Clement Stone, a businessman, philanthropist, and author, wisely said, "I think there is something more important than believing: Action! The world is full of dreamers, and there aren't enough who will move ahead and begin to take concrete steps to actualize their vision." In other words, now is the time to stop procrastination and take action.

As we get close to wrapping up, one of the most common questions we get is, "What now?" In the conclusion, we'll answer this question and share some final thoughts on how to sustain the momentum!

REFLECTION QUESTIONS FOR THIS CHAPTER

1. What is one area of your life you would like to commit more time and effort to?
2. What is one habit you would like to develop, change, or stop?
3. While you read this chapter, what thoughts came to mind regarding your own life (both personal and professional)?
4. How can your vision, roles and goals, and pre-week planning empower you to do what matters most?

CONCLUSION

How to Sustain the Momentum

Initially, we promised that someone who consistently follows the Do What Matters Most habits would see at least a 30 to 50 percent increase in productivity. Now that you're almost finished with the book, can you see and feel how powerful these habits are, especially in this structured approach?

The real question is: What does this all mean for you? In Chapter 8, we illustrated how someone doing pre-week planning accomplished an average of 20 more priorities in a week than they did before pre-week planning. Over a month, that equates to 80 priorities or action items. In a year, that means accomplishing an additional 1,000 priorities or action items that otherwise probably wouldn't have happened—all with less stress. Doing more with less stress is a great recipe for success that most people get excited about!

Imagine the cumulative impact of maintaining these three habits for the rest of your life. Over 40 years, that equates to an additional 40,000+ priorities or activities you will accomplish as a result of these habits, especially the habit of pre-week planning.

On paper, those are numbers. Yet every one of those numbers represents a meaningful activity in your life: exercise, meditation, an act of kindness to your spouse or family member, an important activity related to your job, taking care of something for a client or team member, taking a walk in nature, scheduling a proactive health check-up, or visiting with a friend. The point is that every one of those numbers represents something important to you.

The beauty of the whole process is that your stress and task saturation decrease as you're doing what matters most and accomplishing more. That translates into more peace, happiness, and satisfaction—the things everyone wants in life.

Steve's Journey

None of us knows how long we have in this journey called life, but whatever time we have, we'll likely look back and say it passed us by as if it were a dream. To illustrate this point, we'll share one final, personal example from Steve's life.

At the young age of 55, Steve's wife, Roxanne (Rob's mother), was diagnosed with early-onset Alzheimer's disease. This diagnosis was unexpected and suddenly changed nearly all their long-term plans. Imagine how you would feel if the doctor gave your lifelong partner a diagnosis that would change every one of your "golden year" plans. Early-onset Alzheimer's is a terminal disease that usually takes the patient's life within 10 years of diagnosis.

Indeed, Roxanne passed away after a slow and challenging 10-year decline. During her decade-long battle with this vicious disease, the decline in her cognitive skills and functionality was slow and steady. The family decided to move her to a care center during her last year. At that point, she could barely utter a word, didn't recognize the family, and wholly depended on others for food and care. It was difficult to watch such a fantastic woman slowly deteriorate into someone entirely dependent on people she didn't recognize.

Yet, in this journey that nobody ever wished for, I (Rob) watched my hero father focus on his vision, goals, and pre-week planning. As the caregiver, he could have easily gone to a dark place. However, the combination of his vision, goals, and especially pre-week planning helped him focus on what he could control and what mattered most.

In the early stages, Roxanne and Steve set new goals to travel the world together and make memories while they could. Roxanne accompanied Steve on many of his speaking engagements and corporate training events.

Several years later, when she spent her final months in the care center, she remained Steve's highest priority. Part of his new vision in the role of husband was *Help her feel comfortable and live the final part of her life with honor and dignity.* Every night, he visited Roxanne in the care center and patiently cared for her, treating her like a queen. He would stroke her hand and help her do one of the only things she could do to express herself: smile. He often sat with her and reviewed picture books they created from their trips and time together. The only benefit to Alzheimer's is that every day was new, and they could look at the same pictures as if Roxanne had never seen them. Even though she no longer recognized him, Steve brought her flowers and chocolates and tried to brighten her day.

While caring for Roxanne, he still had to show up in some of his other key roles. He still needed to take care of his own physical and mental health, especially as a caregiver. He was still running several businesses and was involved in multiple organizations. He was still a father to 6 children and a grandfather to 18 grandchildren. He also had responsibilities at his local church. The point is that he would have likely drowned physically and emotionally without his vision, goals, and pre-week planning. How else would he have made time to balance those priorities while still caring for Roxanne?

The big three are about far more than professional success. In Steve's case, he balanced his time between running multiple organizations, spending time with his family, and taking care of his beloved wife of more than 45 years. When Roxanne was diagnosed with Alzheimer's, Steve's vision changed. Rather than focus on the negative, he adjusted his vision and set new goals. We'll be the first to acknowledge that this was one of the hardest things we've ever gone through, which made these critical habits even more important.

Everyone will experience different challenges. For some, the challenge might be health related; for others, it might be relationships or finances. But when we focus on the vision rather than the problem, we're empowered to move forward and get up in the morning with hope and direction.

No matter what curveballs life may throw, these habits will help you make the best of whatever comes your way. So, whether things are great for you right now or you're navigating your own challenges, let's see how Do What Matters Most can help you move forward in your journey.

What Now?

Now that you have finished the book, the most common question is, *What do I do now*, or *How do I sustain the momentum and stick with pre-week planning?*

Here are some of our recommendations:

- **Take or retake the personal productivity self-assessment found at BYBAssessment.com.** If you took the assessment when you started the book, we invite you to retake it after you finish your vision and goals and have been doing pre-week planning for at least one month. An easy way to ensure you do this is to schedule it on your calendar. Consider adding it to your calendar about a month from now and include the website link. At that point, you simply have to go to the website and take the assessment. The other alternative is to redo the circle of peace and balance from Chapter 2. Once you do this, compare where you were at the beginning of this book against where you are after applying the habits; we're confident you will see a positive difference in almost every area of your life!
- **Subscribe to the Do What Matters Most follow-up and accountability emails.** Email Support@BecomingYourBest.com and sign up for the Do What Matters Most emails to get a weekly reminder to do pre-week planning. Additionally, you'll get several tips on how to refine your vision and goals as well as other time management ideas. Everyone who attends a workshop or completes the on-demand course will automatically get these reminders. So, if you have already participated in a course, you should be getting these emails. If not, please check your spam folder or send us an email.

  The idea is to give yourself reminders and touchpoints while developing the habits. These are quick motivation boosts designed to help you stay on track.
- **Get a free podcast.** You can listen to our podcast via iTunes, Stitcher, or any other place that publishes podcasts. Search for the "Becoming Your Best" podcast with Steve and Rob Shallenberger. When you

find it, click Subscribe and you'll get a notification when a new episode is released. For those getting our weekly newsletter, the podcast link will be included. You can also go to the podcast page at BecomingYourBest.com and search through hundreds of podcasts for a topic on your mind.

- **Get the paper or the digital planner for Chrome or Outlook.** Based on our experience, most people who develop the habit of pre-week planning have the appropriate tools. That means getting a paper planner, the digital planner for Chrome or Outlook, or customizing your own planner from our website. You'll be much more successful using one of these planners because you'll have your vision and goals in one place. These planners are designed as a one-stop shop to help you organize your life around your roles. To get your planner or customize your own, visit DoWhatMattersMostPlanner.com.
- **Enroll in a Do What Matters Most online training or on-demand course (self-paced).** Everyone benefits from repetition, regardless of whether your learning style is visual or auditory. It's interesting to hear from people who attended the Do What Matters Most course more than once. They almost always say they got a lot more from it the second time than the first. That makes sense when you think about how the brain processes and learns; we all benefit from repetition because we hear or see things we missed the first time around. A lot of people have family or coworkers who would like to participate. You can also enroll them in the course, and they can go through it for the first time.

  To participate in a live course, visit BecomingYourBest.com and click Learning Options. When there, you can either select a live virtual course or the on-demand course. If your schedule doesn't allow you to join a live course, opt for the on-demand course, and you can go through it at your own pace and on your own schedule.

- **Consider getting certified as a Do What Matters Most trainer or coach.** You can get certified as a Do What Matters Most trainer or coach within your organization. Certification is an excellent approach because you can train people and teams on your cadence and schedule. To get more information on trainer certification, visit BecomingYourBest.com and click Certification from the Learning Options drop-down menu.

- **Customize your own planner.** Although we offer great planning tools in paper and digital planners, as already discussed, you may want to design and customize your own planner. We've developed a site that allows you to customize your entire planner—from the cover to the inside pages, it's all built for you, by you. To learn more, go to DoWhatMattersMostPlanner.com and choose the option to design your planner.
- **Finish a draft of your vision and roles and goals, and then commit to pre-week planning.** If you haven't already done it, consider doing the following right now while it's fresh in your mind:
    - Schedule a time on your calendar to finalize your vision and goals. Once they're finished, add them to your planner.
    - Schedule a time in your calendar each week when you think you'll most likely do pre-week planning. Make sure the reminder is set to repeat each week, perhaps on a quiet Saturday or Sunday morning. Scheduling pre-week planning will increase the likelihood of consistency, even if you don't do it at the scheduled time.
- **Hold a weekly alignment meeting with your team.** If you're in a leadership capacity, this is one of the most important things you can do as a leader. We suggest you hold this meeting on Monday while the entire week is in front of you. The point of this meeting is to get aligned on what matters most as a team this week. The meeting will be significantly better if each team member has already done their pre-week planning before the meeting. You can carry the same idea into the family. If applicable, you could meet as a family on Sunday evening to review the week and ensure you're all aligned.

Wrap Up

Congratulations on finishing Do What Matters Most!

But this isn't the end; it's just the beginning. The art is in the start, and now is the time to start. As Zig Ziglar said, "You don't have to be great to start, but you have to start to be great."

Developing these habits will be a journey that transforms every area of your personal and professional life—as it has for us and thousands of others.

We invite you to share this book with your coworkers, friends, and family members so they can develop their vision and goals, and learn how to do pre-week planning. We also invite you to share your story by emailing us at Support@BecomingYourBest.com. We would love to hear about your experience with the process.

Ella Wheeler Wilcox, a famous author and poet from the late 1800s, expressed a thought that applies to all of us:

> *One ship [sails] east and another west, with the selfsame winds that blow. 'Tis the set of the sail, and not the gale, that [determines] the way [they'll] go. Like the winds of the sea are the ways of fate; as we voyage along through life, 'Tis the set of a soul, that decides its goal, and not the calm or the strife.*[1]

In the spirit of Wilcox's quote, a figurative wind blows at your back. The question is: How will you choose to set your sail to catch it?

With the Do What Matters Most program and habits, you're empowered to lead a life by design rather than by default. You have a structured approach to make the best of your dash and prioritize what matters most week in and week out, even when things don't go as planned.

These habits help us all hoist and set our sails, catch the wind, and do what matters most!

DO WHAT MATTERS MOST DISCUSSION GUIDE

We hope the three high-performance habits shared in *Do What Matters Most* have had a significant impact on your life. As you read throughout the book, the promise is that these habits will increase productivity by at least 30 to 50 percent and, more importantly, empower you to prioritize your time and do what matters most!

These discussion questions are meant to summarize the book and should be considered from an individual and team level.

INDIVIDUALS

1. From your circle of peace and balance, what areas of your personal and professional life would you like to improve?
2. Using the Do What Matters Most matrix, what quadrant do you spend most of your time in personally and professionally? Why?
3. Because we have all been in different quadrants at different times, how would you describe the emotions associated with each quadrant?
4. What is the difference in feeling between Q2 and every other quadrant?
5. How would a guiding personal vision positively affect your life?
6. The book contains four questions designed to fire up your imagination before you write your vision. How would you answer each of these?

   A. In 5 to 10 years, what are some things you want to do and accomplish?

   B. Think of any mentors or people who have inspired you (these can be people you know personally or historical figures). What traits or characteristics do you admire about them?

C. What would you like to improve in your job, home, or community?

D. Fifty years from today, whether you are alive or not, how do you hope others will look back and describe you?

7. What are your five to seven most important roles (personal/self, job title, parent, spouse/partner, brother/sister, son/daughter, friend, church member, caretaker, etc.)? Remember, personal or self is the most important role!
8. What is your vision for each role?
9. What were your thoughts and feelings while developing your vision?
10. Where will you put your personal vision so that you can reference it each week as part of pre-week planning?
11. What are one to four goals (by role) for this year that support your vision?
12. What was the experience of developing your roles and goals like for you?
13. Who are three to five people with whom you could share your goals to increase accountability?
14. Who else do you know who would benefit from developing their vision and goals?
15. How can pre-week planning help you prioritize your time and do what matters most?
16. When is the best time to allocate 20 to 50 minutes to do pre-week planning? Have you set a reminder on your phone or calendar?
17. Have you visited DoWhatMattersMostPlanner.com and invested in a planner? You can choose a pre-designed planner, download a digital planner for Chrome or Outlook, or customize your own planner. Which do you think is the best approach for your long-term success?
18. How can this program and its tools empower you to do what matters most? In other words, how will they improve your life?

TEAM

1. What is the current mindset and culture within your team?
2. How do you measure performance and productivity?
3. What can each team member do to be a better contributor or leader?
4. How can your team be more aligned around a compelling vision?
5. What would be the impact on your team if each person had a written personal vision?
6. Does your team members' and coworkers' personal visions align with their role and the organization's vision? If so, great. If not, why?
7. How does your team feel about goal setting?
8. How many team members currently have specific, measurable goals for the month, quarter, or year?
9. How often do you or your team review your goals?
10. How can the goals be worded to eliminate terms like *more* or *better*? In other words, how can they be phrased in a way that creates a clear target?
11. How do your team members or coworkers prioritize their time to do what matters most?
12. How can pre-week planning help your team members or coworkers improve their focus on what matters most?
13. If each person reviewed their monthly, quarterly, or annual goals each week as part of pre-week planning, what impact would it have on the team?
14. Is there a team member you could join up with as an accountability partner to develop the habit of pre-week planning each week?
15. How aligned is your team currently? How could pre-week planning help each individual be more aligned with what matters most?
16. Are you already holding a weekly alignment meeting at the beginning of the week? If not, when could you?

17. If you could wave a magic wand and improve one aspect of your team, what would it be?
18. How can Do What Matters Most help your coworkers or team members increase performance and productivity?

NOTES

Chapter 1

1 Henry Mintzberg, "The Manager's Job: Folklore and Fact," *Harvard Business Review*, July–August 1975, https://hbr.org/1990/03/the-managers-job-folklore-and-fact.

2 Carol Dweck, *Mindset: The New Psychology of Success* (New York: Random House, 2006).

3 Og Mandino, *The Greatest Salesman in the World* (New York: Bantam Books, 1968), 47.

Chapter 2

1 Harvard School of Public Health, "The Good Life: A Discussion with Dr. Robert Waldinger," February 27, 2023, https://www.hsph.harvard.edu/health-happiness/2023/02/27/the-good-life-a-discussion-with-dr-robert-waldinger/.

2 Jim Harter, "Employee Engagement on the Rise in the U.S.," Gallup, August 26, 2018, https://news.gallup.com/poll/241649/employee-engagement-rise.aspx.

3 Integra, "IRR Sponsored Study: 'Desk Rage' and Workplace Stress," Integra Realty Resources, November 29, 2000, https://www.irr.com/news/irr-sponsored-study-desk-rage-and-workplace-stress-9677.

4 Harter, "Employee Engagement on the Rise in the U.S."

5 Kermit Pattison, "Worker, Interrupted: The Cost of Task Switching," *Fast Company*, July 28, 2008, https://www.fastcompany.com/944128/worker-interrupted-cost-task-switching.

6 Becoming Your Best Global Leadership, Performance and Productivity Survey, 2018–2019.

Chapter 4

1 Tom Benson, "Re-Living the Wright Way: Biography of Orville Wright," National Aeronautics and Space Administration, last modified June 12, 2014, 05:10, https://web.archive.org/web/20220418151012/https://wright.nasa.gov/orville.htm.

2 Wikipedia, "Wright Flyer," Wikimedia Foundation, last modified October 23, 2020, https://en.wikipedia.org/wiki/Wright_Flyer.
3 Jim Collins, *Good to Great: Why Some Companies Make the Leap . . . and Others Don't* (New York: HarperCollins, 2001), 42.

Chapter 5

1 Zig Ziglar, *Over the Top: Moving from Survival to Stability, from Stability to Success, from Success to Significance* (Nashville: Thomas Nelson, 1994).
2 James Allen, "Visions and Ideals," in *As a Man Thinketh* (Chicago: Sheldon University Press, 1908), 86.

Chapter 6

1 Les Brown, *Live Your Dreams* (New York: Quill, 2001), 105–106.
2 Lewis Carroll, *Alice's Adventures in Wonderland*, Chapter 6, last updated October 12, 2020, https://www.gutenberg.org/files/11/11-h/11-h.htm.

Chapter 7

1 Shivali Best, "Day That People Most Likely to Give Up Their New Year's Resolutions—And It's Very Soon," *The Mirror*, January 2, 2020, https://www.mirror.co.uk/science/day-people-most-likely-give-21199904.
2 Og Mandino, *The Greatest Salesman in the World* (New York: Bantam Books, 1968), 67.

Chapter 10

1 Jon Peddie Research, "Jon Peddie Research: Multiple Displays Can Increase Productivity by 42%," JPR, October 26, 2017, https://www.jonpeddie.com/press-releases/jon-peddie-research-multiple-displays-can-increase-productivity-by-42/.

Conclusion

1 Ella Wheeler Wilcox, *World Voices* (New York: Hearst's International Library Company, 1916).

ACKNOWLEDGMENTS

We are deeply grateful to the people who invested so much time and effort to help with the research, editing, and organization of *Do What Matters Most*. We want to highlight some of the people who have been instrumental in helping publish this book.

Thank you to the members of the amazing team at Becoming Your Best who have been with us for years doing a lot of the behind-the-scenes work: Jamie Thorup, Clayton Snyder, Thomas Blackwell, Hanna Fabrizio, Tommy Shallenberger, Laura Shallenberger, and Anne Petersen.

Thank you to the incredible team at Berrett-Koehler for your wise counsel, recommendations, and efforts. There were many people involved in the design team, marketing team, and editorial committees. We wanted to especially thank Steve Piersanti, Jeevan Sivasubramaniam, Ashley Ingram, Rachel Monaghan, and Maureen Forys.

To those who provided edits, proofreads, recommendations, and new ideas, thank you! Mark Holland, Gary Marlowe, Sue Muehlbach, William Thompson, Kerry Mitchell, Mike Choutka, Melanie Wong, John Jeppson, Suzanne Oliver, Pat Do, Zach Gajewski, Josh Vahovius, Jeff Arnold, Max Ganado, Bruce Matulich, Jean Henri Lhuillier, Terry Grant, Minal Shah, Bobby Gadhia, Noel Otto, Emery Rubagenga, Dan Cantaragiu, Reuben Xuereb, David Xuereb, Charles Spalding, Raul Arizpe, Thibault Relecom, Jody Richards, Erin Galyean, Rick Taylor, Erick McHenry, Jassim Alharoon, Sulaiman Altehaini, Abdulaziz Alahmadi, Abdullah Al-Sharif, and Melanie Gentry.

We also want to acknowledge and thank some of the key mentors and influencers who have had a big impact on our lives: David Clark, Cal Clark, David Conger, Robert Dellenbach, William Jones, Thomas Monson, Stephen Covey, Gardner Russell, Lael Woodbury, and our wonderful friends at Synergy Companies.

For our family members, you have been the backbone and support who give us the ability to work on these kinds of projects. Thank you to Roxanne, David, Steven, Tommy, Daniel, and Anne (and each of their amazing spouses)! In addition, thank you to Tonya, Robbie, Bella, Lana, and Clara. We love every one of you and hope you will share the habits in this book with future generations.

Above all, we want to acknowledge God as the source of inspiration and guidance throughout the years. We believe these principles and habits are divinely inspired and will help people and organizations achieve the very best versions of themselves!

INDEX

Q

R

ABOUT THE AUTHORS

Rob Shallenberger

Rob has always been intrigued by adventure and had a drive to challenge himself. After graduating from Utah State University and earning an MBA from Colorado State University, he became a fighter pilot in the United States Air Force. During his time in the Air Force, Rob was also an Advance Agent for Air Force One. This was an exciting time because he could work with foreign embassies, the Secret Service, and the White House staff.

As an F-16 pilot and Air Force One Advance Agent, Rob experienced firsthand what a high-performance culture looked like. In that world, the standard is perfection, yet the perfect flight has yet to happen. So, an integral part of the culture was the debrief. In the debrief, the pilots would develop lessons learned to repeat successes and eliminate failures and mistakes. Part of the fighter pilot culture is that when a pilot is tasked with something, they do it right and on time. Rob found this high-performance culture fun, exciting, and results-focused. What makes the fighter pilot culture elite are the people and the extensive training that aligns processes and efforts!

Rob wanted to bring this same high-performance culture to organizations, so it was the perfect match for him to partner with his father, who had already researched high performance for decades. Together, Rob and Steve founded Becoming Your Best Global Leadership and continued the research, which culminated, initially, in the release of their first book, *Becoming Your Best: The 12 Principles of Highly Successful Leaders*. Following the release of *Becoming Your Best*, they went on to author five other books, including *Start with the Vision: The Six Steps to Effectively Plan, Create Solutions, and Take Action*; *Conquer Anxiety*; and *How to Succeed in High School* (for teenagers and their parents).

Rob considers it an honor to have personally trained hundreds of organizations around the world. He loves to hear stories about how these habits have transformed lives, both personally and professionally.

Rob's primary focus is on his faith and family. He's been married for 27 years and has four children.

Steve Shallenberger

After graduating from Brigham Young University with a degree in accounting, Steve bought his first company at 26 years old. It quickly grew, and before he knew it, the company had more than 700 employees. Many of the employees were sales reps who traveled around the country each summer selling books, videos, and other products.

It was common for the managers or sales reps to ask him, "What principles or habits should I focus on to be among the best?" At the time, Steve had a few ideas, but the more he thought about that question, the more he realized that there had to be a better answer. Thus, he started his journey researching great leaders and high performers to determine what set them apart from everyone else. Identifying the 12 principles of highly successful people and leaders was the culmination of 40 years of research.

Steve and Rob started Becoming Your Best Global Leadership based on that research. Their focus is on helping organizations develop high-performing people and teams that know how to focus on what matters most. HR.com named Becoming Your Best Global Leadership one of the top three global leadership programs, and it continues to win awards for the high-caliber training and impact it is having on leadership, time management, and productivity.

Steve has had the opportunity to train organizations worldwide. He is constantly reminded that while we are diverse in many ways, the foundations of personal and professional success—the big three habits shared in this book—transcend race, culture, and gender.

Throughout his life, Steve has been a part of several organizations that have had a deep impact on him and his research. He graduated from the Harvard Business School Owner/President Management (OPM) program and has been influenced by many of his peers, whom he continues to associate with decades later. He has also been a part of the Young Presidents Organization (YPO) for more than 40 years; the relationships, adventures, and experiences with YPO have influenced many aspects of Steve's life.

He was married for 46 years until his beloved wife, Roxanne, passed away from early-onset Alzheimer's disease. He loves spending time with his 6 children and 21 grandchildren.

ABOUT BECOMING YOUR BEST GLOBAL LEADERSHIP

Becoming Your Best Global Leadership is a top-rated leadership training company that offers a suite of award-winning training solutions. Its training is delivered through live and virtual keynotes, certification, workshops, and coaching to transform people and empower public and private organizations to create a culture by design.

Becoming Your Best specializes in the following areas:

- Leadership
- Time-management, work–life balance, and productivity
- Planning and problem solving
- Strategic planning and alignment

In 2018, Becoming Your Best won an award for "Best Global Leadership Program" from HR.com for its measured training results and the impact it had in organizations. Our standard is that whether the training is delivered by one of our master trainers or a certified trainer within your organization, productivity and performance will increase by an average of 30 to 50 percent because of our proprietary time management tools and processes! Those results can be expected from executives, managers, and frontline team members.

Becoming Your Best's first book, *Becoming Your Best: The 12 Principles of Highly Successful Leaders*, is a national bestseller and was founded on 40 years of research to identify what set apart the top 10 percent of great leaders and high performers across industries. Of course, nobody we researched was perfect (none of us are), but when we saw what high performers focused on, the 12 principles were clearly the common denominator of success among them.

Based on the 12 principles, Becoming Your Best established the foundation of its award-winning leadership training and has trained hundreds of public and private organizations around the world.

The next book released was *Start with the Vision: Six Steps to Effectively Plan, Create Solutions, and Take Action*. In our ongoing research, we found that only 10 percent of organizations have a planning or problem-solving process that is used across the team and/or organization. The six-step process brings teams and organizations together with a common language and planning process to address any issue, saving them countless hours and a significant amount of money while fostering imagination and collaboration.

This book, *Do What Matters Most*, will close the time management and productivity gap that so many people and organizations experience. The Do What Matters Most training and certification are life-changing and empower team members to focus on three high-performance habits that less than 1 percent of people do! Additionally, it helps team members improve their physical and mental well-being, work–life balance, and relationships.

Companies such as Charles Schwab, PepsiCo, the Dallas Cowboys, and many others have completed this training with impressive results. In addition to Fortune 500 companies, small startups and large government organizations have also experienced how effective the Becoming Your Best training is with their people and teams. We have licensed partners and certified corporate trainers throughout the world, and we are continually expanding into more countries.

Our Vision

The vision for Becoming Your Best Global Leadership is to add lasting value to people and organizations and to positively impact a billion lives. Reaching one billion people is an understandably lofty vision that will take years, maybe even decades.

One key to achieving this vision is using simple, fun, and scalable content and training that has a tremendous impact on personal and professional results. In addition, accomplishing this vision will happen exponentially faster when certified trainers spread this results-focused training widely and deeply throughout their own organizations.

We invite you and your organization to join us in this vision of positively impacting a billion lives!

For questions about trainer certification, keynotes, workshops, or other training, please email us at Support@BecomingYourBest.com, call us at 888-690-8764, or visit our website at BecomingYourBest.com.

Berrett–Koehler
Publishers

Berrett-Koehler is an independent publisher dedicated to an ambitious mission: *Connecting people and ideas to create a world that works for all.*

Our publications span many formats, including print, digital, audio, and video. We also offer online resources, training, and gatherings. And we will continue expanding our products and services to advance our mission.

We believe that the solutions to the world's problems will come from all of us, working at all levels: in our society, in our organizations, and in our own lives. Our publications and resources offer pathways to creating a more just, equitable, and sustainable society. They help people make their organizations more humane, democratic, diverse, and effective (and we don't think there's any contradiction there). And they guide people in creating positive change in their own lives and aligning their personal practices with their aspirations for a better world.

And we strive to practice what we preach through what we call "The BK Way." At the core of this approach is *stewardship,* a deep sense of responsibility to administer the company for the benefit of all of our stakeholder groups, including authors, customers, employees, investors, service providers, sales partners, and the communities and environment around us. Everything we do is built around stewardship and our other core values of *quality, partnership, inclusion,* and *sustainability.*

This is why Berrett-Koehler is the first book publishing company to be both a B Corporation (a rigorous certification) and a benefit corporation (a for-profit legal status), which together require us to adhere to the highest standards for corporate, social, and environmental performance. And it is why we have instituted many pioneering practices (which you can learn about at www.bkconnection.com), including the Berrett-Koehler Constitution, the Bill of Rights and Responsibilities for BK Authors, and our unique Author Days.

We are grateful to our readers, authors, and other friends who are supporting our mission. We ask you to share with us examples of how BK publications and resources are making a difference in your lives, organizations, and communities at www.bkconnection.com/impact.

Dear reader,

Thank you for picking up this book and welcome to the worldwide BK community! You're joining a special group of people who have come together to create positive change in their lives, organizations, and communities.

What's BK all about?

Our mission is to connect people and ideas to create a world that works for all.

Why? Our communities, organizations, and lives get bogged down by old paradigms of self-interest, exclusion, hierarchy, and privilege. But we believe that can change. That's why we seek the leading experts on these challenges—and share their actionable ideas with you.

A welcome gift

To help you get started, we'd like to offer you a **free copy** of one of our bestselling ebooks:

www.bkconnection.com/welcome

When you claim your **free ebook**, you'll also be subscribed to our blog.

Our freshest insights

Access the best new tools and ideas for leaders at all levels on our blog at ideas.bkconnection.com.

Sincerely,

Your friends at Berrett-Koehler